Science Notebooks

Science Notebooks
Writing About Inquiry

Brian Campbell and Lori Fulton

Foreword by Linda Gregg

HEINEMANN
Portsmouth, NH

Heinemann

361 Hanover Street
Portsmouth, NH 03801–3912
www.heinemann.com

Offices and agents throughout the world

Library of Congress Cataloging-in-Publication Data
Campbell, Brian, 1974–
    Science notebooks : writing about inquiry / Brian Campbell and Lori Fulton ; foreword by Linda Gregg.
        p. cm.
    Includes bibliographical references.
    ISBN 0-325-00568-0 (alk. paper)
    1. Science—Study and teaching (Elementary)—United States.   2. School notebooks—United States.
3. Learning by discovery.   I. Fulton, Lori.   II. Title.

LB1585.3.C36 2003
372.3'5—dc21

                                                                                        2003006679

Editor: Robin Najar
Production: Vicki Kasabian
Cover design: Joni Doherty
Typesetter: Kim Arney Mulcahy
Manufacturing: Steve Bernier

Printed in the United States of America on acid-free paper

12 11 10   VP   13 14 15

*We would like to thank all those who supported us
and assisted us in our endeavor,
especially*

Stephanie Campbell

Leanne Fernald

Alan Gallaspy

Linda Gregg

Bonnie Pillaro

Kay Rohde

And, most important, all the children
with whom we have ever worked.

Contents

Foreword *by Linda Gregg* / xiii

Introduction 1

Provides an overview of the book, including the goals of the book, a guide on how to use it as a resource, an explanation of the science notebook, and a brief description of each chapter.

1 The Role of the Teacher 5

This chapter examines what factors teachers need to think about before, during, and after implementation of science notebooks.

    Planning / 5

    Implementation of Science Notebooks / 11

    Formative Assessment / 16

    Developing Science Notebooks / 17

    Creating a Purpose for Notebooks / 22

2 Elements of a Science Notebook 25

This chapter details important aspects that are included in a science notebook and shares strategies to develop them further.

    Recording and Organizing Data / 25

    Technical Drawings / 31

    Students' Questions / 36

    Recording Thinking / 39

    Other Elements / 44

3 **Signs of Student Progress** **48**

This chapter examines how students progress in their use of science note-books both during and after an investigation.

    Predicting / 48

    Recording and Organizing Data / 50

    Drawing / 51

    Questioning / 53

    Reflecting / 54

    Using Notebooks as a Resource / 55

    Self-Assessing / 56

4 **Discussions with Two Scientists** **57**

This chapter shares two scientists' thoughts on the role and importance of notebooks in their work as well as implications for the use of notebooks in the classroom.

    How Scientists Use Their Notebooks / 57

    Recommendations for the Classroom / 60

5 **Scientific Content and Process Connections** **64**

This chapter examines how the science notebook aids in conceptual development of scientific concepts.

    Connections to the *National Science Education Standards* / 64

    Physical, Life, and Earth and Space Content Standards / 65

    Science as Inquiry / 67

    Unifying Concepts and Processes / 70

6 **Literacy Connections** **73**

This chapter explores how the science notebook can be used as a context for developing literacy.

    Connections to Literacy / 73

    Oral Communication / 73

Written Communication / 75

Reading / 77

Vocabulary Development / 79

Connections to the *Standards for the English Language Arts* / 80

Appendix / 83

Bibliography / 93

*An important stage of inquiry and of student science learning is the oral
and written discourse that focuses the attention of students on how they know what
they know and how their knowledge connects to larger ideas,
other domains, and the world beyond the classroom.*

National Research Council, National Science Education Standards

We tried to filter the material from the water with a screen. Only gravel worked.

Water and earth would not seperate. I guess the fibers are too thin. The salt certainly didn't come out, it had already dissolved.

Going to try filtering with a funnel. Gravel worked again.

Salt worked too & the water was purified and the salt got stuck in the water. Now for earth.

Waiting... Catherine

Foreword

Lori Fulton and Brian Campbell began their inquiry into how to help teachers use science notebooks to help children learn science more than four years ago as learners themselves. Both were participants in the Science Inquiry Institute, led by Dr. Becky Dyasi and Mitch Bleier. Participants in the institute kept individual science notebooks to record all aspects of their science inquiries. Following the institute, twelve participants began a study group on science notebooks. Lori facilitated the group, which met for a school semester.

Four teacher leaders continued to meet during the next two years, bringing student notebooks to share and supporting one another as they each worked to understand how to use science notebooks to promote student learning. Brian came to the study group with samples of student work and stories about how valuable writing seemed to be for his students: second graders who many did not expect would be able to record their findings with such detail. Other teachers also brought student work. They studied the students' notebooks, exchanging stories and questions. Then they shaped and refined productive questions to investigate within their classrooms.

Lori and Brian began talking to scientists to see how they used notebooks, examining the parallels with student use of notebooks. Lori shared what they were finding with teacher leaders who had visited Pasadena Unified School District in California, where Jennifer Yure, K–12 science specialist, was implementing a strong science notebook component as part of the science program. The work in Pasadena served as a model of districtwide use of science notebooks.

Lori and Brian continued to search for other resources to learn more about science notebooks, but in fact, they were learning from their work with children and teachers. The more they learned, the more questions they had and the greater their expertise became. They began to encourage teachers to keep science notebooks in the professional development sessions that they designed and facilitated. Lori also began working in classrooms with teachers who were just beginning to use science notebooks with their students as a result of using notebooks when they attended professional development sessions. The charm of the students' work and their pride in ownership of the knowledge recorded in their notebooks motivated teachers to move into unknown territory. The teachers worked together figuring out how to create time and authentic reasons for students to record the stories of their investigations and how to best have students use their notebooks to share their findings.

Over time, more and more teachers and administrators began to consider notebooks an important part of their science programs. Teachers and administrators were beginning to share stories about student writing that communicated increased understanding of the science content they were studying and the processes of inquiry they were using. Teachers began to describe how students were referring to their notebooks when sharing their findings and questioning their peers.

In this book, Lori and Brian share the questions that they asked and questions that other teachers asked. They present their findings and current thinking about science notebooks. At the same time, they continue to question and learn more about science notebooks.

You are invited to join them on this journey. See what happens when you ask your own questions as you observe your students growing as writers and learners. Listen closely to student conversations. Begin your own notebook and share with your colleagues. Will students benefit if you share your writings with them? Will you benefit from learning to record what you are thinking and learning about maintaining a science notebook? Will recording your ideas enrich your teaching practices and extend your learning? What impact on your teaching and learning will forming a study group with colleagues to share student notebooks have? What will happen when you reflect on your findings? On how you ask questions and plan your next steps in teaching and learning?

As you use this book, enjoy the opportunity to help students learn to write and talk about their thinking. Welcome the invitation the book provides to ask questions and learn from and with your students. As you help your students learn and collect evidence to support their ideas, think about what *you* are learning. Give the process of implementing science notebooks a realistic test. Be adventurous when considering ideas and strategies that may be different than those you have used before. Collect evidence about what you do and what you see students doing. Be willing to give yourself and your students time to learn to write as scientists write, to share thinking, and to support ideas with evidence that has been collected in notebooks. Help students learn to respectfully question each other and to question what they hear and read. Explore how much you will learn about your students from their writing and verbal communication.

Let *Science Notebooks* guide you as you question and rethink how, when, and why to use science notebooks. You may find that reading the vignettes in this book and writing your own vignettes about what is happening in your classroom become a window into your own learning and generate questions about the learning environment you are creating. The ideas presented in *Science Notebooks* will support, extend, and enrich learning for your students, yourself, and your learning community.

The power of writing is evident in the story of this book. As Lori and Brian continued to question, field-test their ideas, and write the chapters to share their thinking and findings, their ideas became more clearly focused and articulated. As I interacted with them over the years, my thinking continued to be enriched and refreshed. It is an honor to write this foreword for a work that will contribute to the art and practice of teaching and learning, one written by two educators dedicated to asking productive questions and sharing their findings as well as their passion for science inquiry and science notebooks.

Linda Gregg
Former Coordinator, Mathematics and Science Services,
Curriculum and Professional Development Division,
Clark County School District
Director, Investigations Implementation Center,
TERC

Science Notebooks

Introduction

What is the purpose of this book?

The purpose of science notebooks is to build science content and process skills in a manner similar to the way scientists work, while serving as a context for developing literacy. The main emphasis of this book is to begin teachers on a journey in developing the use of science notebooks in their elementary classrooms. For those already on this journey, the purpose is to aid in the overall development of notebooks. This book is not designed as a step-by-step guide, but as a resource to develop strategies and methods to make notebooks more meaningful.

Who is the audience of this book?

This book is primarily written for elementary classroom teachers using hands-on, inquiry-based science, which allows for more opportunities to utilize the information presented. However, preservice teachers, middle school science and literacy teachers, administrators, reading specialists, and English language learner facilitators may benefit from various sections as well.

What are science notebooks?

Science notebooks are a natural complement to kit-based programs in which students are actively engaged with materials, involved in small- and whole-group discussions, and using expository text as a reference to confirm or extend ideas after investigations. In the elementary school classroom, science notebooks are a record of students' findings, questions, thoughts, procedures, data, and wonderings that may or may not retell the journey of their science experience.

Science notebooks are

- tools for students to use during science.
- tattered—a sign of regular use—with water stains and bent corners.

- always nearby children, tucked under their arms or close at hand, so they can record a moment in time as they work with the materials.
- personal to the owners and may make sense only to them.
- places to record data, observations, illustrations, understandings, questions, reflections, and ideas while working.
- reference tools students use as they continue their work or talk with others in small- or whole-group discussions.

What can be used as a science notebook?

- a composition book
- a spiral notebook
- a three-ring binder
- a three-prong paper folder
- folded paper

What is the difference among science journals, logs, and notebooks?

As science notebooks gain in popularity, more and more people are using some sort of recording device in their classrooms. Teachers often refer to them as science journals or logs, as well as notebooks. While teachers may use these words interchangeably, the differences among them have led many people to question how others are using these recording devices.

Being familiar with journals in other subject areas, some teachers ask their students to keep journals in science as well. Journals often serve as reflections of students' learning. In science, journals are kept in the desk during the investigation and used only after the work is done and the materials are put away. Most entries usually begin with "Today in science I. . . ." In this sense, journals contain reflections of students' work and not necessarily the data from their investigations.

When teachers refer to logs, they often mean books where students keep data over time. In science, logs are utilized during investigations but are not used during discussions. Students may look back at the data but do not reflect on their understandings or synthesize the data.

Notebooks are meant to be tools for students to record both their data and thinking as they work with materials. They are utilized prior to the investigation to record the students' thinking or planning; during the investigation to record words, pictures, photos, or numbers, possibly getting wet and messy in the process; and after the investigation to help students reflect on their thinking and data in order to share them with others.

How is this book to be used?

This book is designed as a reference for the classroom teacher. The first three chapters focus on classroom implementation, while the last three chapters provide rationale for using notebooks. The chapters are divided into sections that are more meaningful at various stages of notebook development. These sections should be read as needed to help teachers meet their goals in developing science notebooks in the classroom. Within certain sections are vignettes (short stories). These vignettes are based upon the authors' experiences when working with children in a variety of settings utilizing science notebooks. Thinking points are presented throughout the chapters and are designed to help link the ideas presented in this book to the classroom and philosophical beliefs. The thinking points should be revisited from time to time as thinking may change as teachers gain experience with notebooks.

What does the teacher do?

Chapter 1 focuses on the role of the teacher in implementing science notebooks, sharing ideas of how to get authentic notebooks started, and ways to develop them further without infringing upon their authenticity. The chapter also examines ways to purposefully use notebooks in order to help children see them as important tools in their science learning as well as the role they play in helping the teacher make instructional decisions.

What is in a science notebook?

Chapter 2 explores the elements of science notebooks and looks closely at what notebooks might look like. Ideas are presented for helping students record and organize their data using both words and drawings, and the importance of questioning is examined. The chapter also explores how to take students beyond simply recording data to synthesizing their thoughts before, during, and after an investigation.

What are signs of students' progress?

Chapter 3 examines how students progress as they utilize science notebooks. It focuses on students' progress from beginning to more advanced stages in predicting, recording and organizing, drawing, questioning, reflecting, using notebooks as resources, and self-assessing.

What does the scientific community have to say about science notebooks?

Chapter 4 shares conversations with scientists. Since notebooks are an important component of the scientific world, this chapter discusses what are considered important elements of notebooks, and examines how scientists use them in their line of work.

How do notebooks support implementation of the *National Science Education Standards?*

Chapter 5 examines how notebooks can foster the development of scientific content and discusses the implications on students' learning. Connections to the *National Science Education Standards* are shared.

How do science notebooks promote literacy development?

Chapter 6 discusses the use of science notebooks as a context for literacy development. Connections are made between science notebooks and the *Standards for the English Language Arts.*

1

The Role of the Teacher

Planning

Where to begin?

There are certain decisions to make before beginning to use science notebooks in the classroom.

- What type of notebook should be used?
- What should be included with every notebook entry?
- What will students write about in their notebooks?
- What organizational tools will students need?
- Which experience will provide students with a meaningful starting point?

What type of notebook should be used?

To begin, the teacher must decide the physical structure of the science notebook. There are a variety of options, including composition books, spiral notebooks, three-ring binders, two-pocket folders with prongs, or pieces of folded paper stapled with or without a cover. Preference on the type of notebook varies; however, many have found that the composition book allows students to keep a running record of the work and thinking they do throughout the year and represents growth over time. Using a composition book provides ample flexibility for first-time use. Samples that appear in this book come from students who used composition books.

Thinking point: What type of notebook will you use?

What should be included with every notebook entry?

Another decision the teacher must consider is what information will be recorded with each entry; scientists often record the date, time, and weather. These items may not seem important in elementary science; however, by including this information in every entry, students are establishing habits of scientific documentation. Many teachers find it helpful for themselves and their students if a subject or title is included with each entry. This becomes a quick reference to locate information as students flip through their notebooks during discussion.

> *Thinking point:* What information will you expect students to include in all entries?

What will students write about in their notebooks?

Notebooks provide a medium in which students document scientific investigations. It is the responsibility of the teacher to determine what is appropriate for the students to record. For example, it may be more realistic to expect drawings from first graders than the use of Venn diagrams. Chapter 2, "Elements of a Science Notebook," offers a variety of ideas for recording at different grade levels. It may take time before students begin to utilize many of the elements, so it is important to have reasonable expectations. Beginning entries may appear discouraging. Figures 1–1 through 1–4 show beginning entries from students at four different grade levels. Some students may draw smiley faces on animals and write that their insect likes them. This should be expected, as students are most familiar and comfortable with that form of writing or drawing. Students

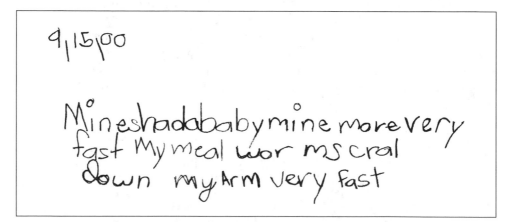

FIGURE 1–1   Beginning notebook entry of a second grader

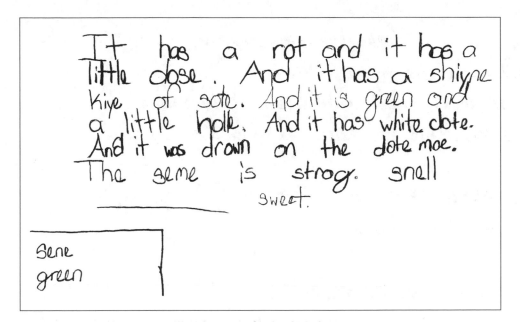

It has a rot and it has a little dose. And it has a shiyne kiye of sote. And it is green and a little holle. And it has white dote. And it was drown on the dote moe. The geme is strog. snell sweet.

Sene green

FIGURE 1–2   Beginning notebook entry of a third grader

will get better as they continue to work with notebooks and use them in their discussions with others. The more students use their notebooks, the more accurate their representations become. Students develop at different rates and their notebooks are no exception. Some students may take to their notebooks right away, recording in great detail, while other students may require extensive support in order to become proficient.

Thinking point: What are realistic expectations for your students' writing?

What organizational tools will students need?

In the beginning it may be necessary to talk with students about organizing their notebooks in a useful manner. One technique that may help with organization is the use of colored tabs. For example, a red tab could mark the section on insects and a yellow tab may signify the solids and liquids section. It may also be helpful to talk with students about using the next blank page rather than skipping around in their notebooks or using an entire page to record information rather than putting only one piece of information on a page. While these may sound like simple ideas, some students struggle with organizational skills, and such techniques may require direction in the form of guiding questions, minilessons, or modeling from both teachers and students.

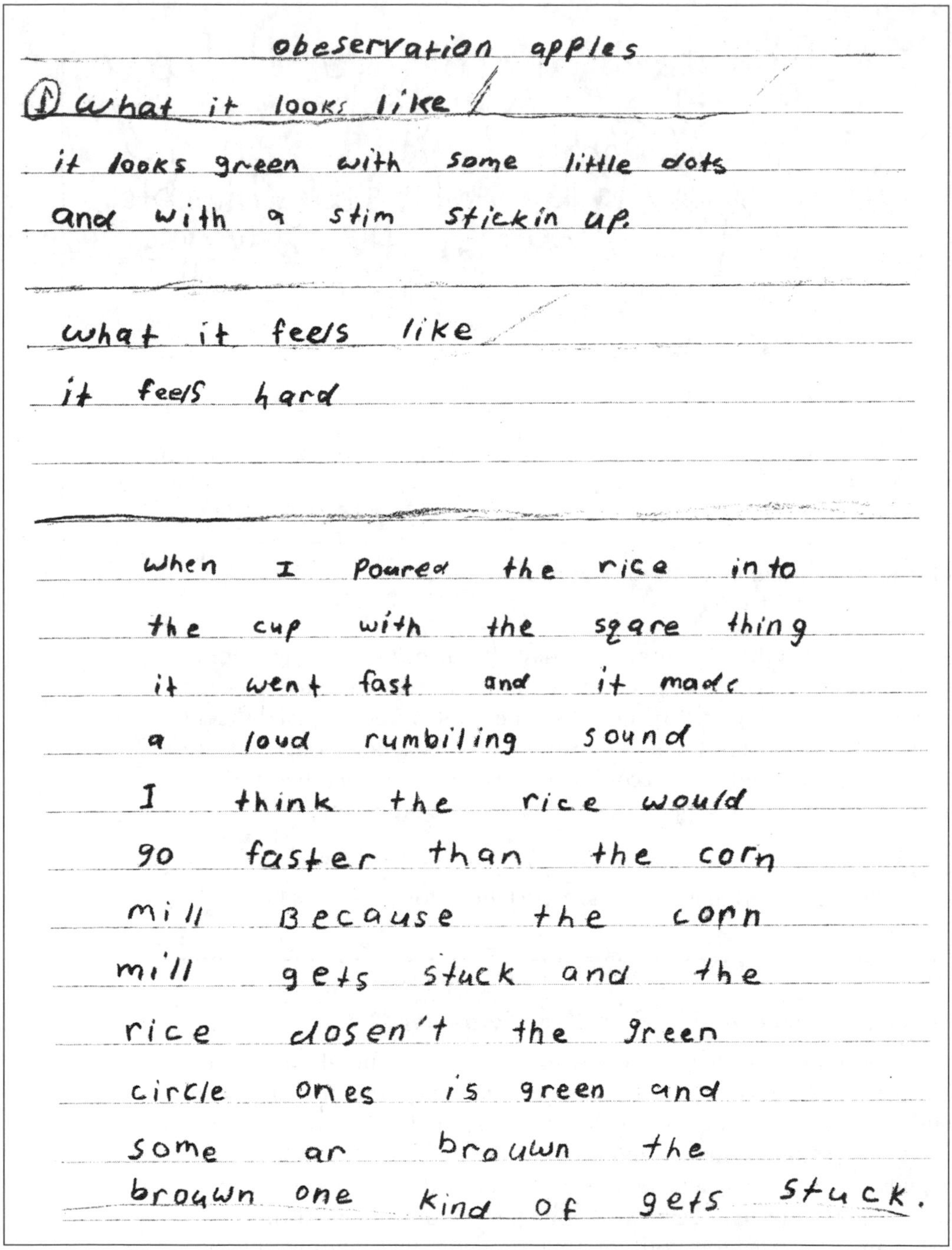

obeservation apples

① What it looks like

it looks green with some little dots
and with a stim stickin up.

what it feels like

it feels hard

when   I   poured   the   rice   into
the   cup   with   the   sqare   thing
it   went   fast   and   it   made
a   loud   rumbiling   sound
I   think   the   rice   would
go   faster   than   the   corn
mill   Because   the   corn
mill   gets   stuck   and   the
rice   dosen't   the   green
circle   ones   is   green   and
some   ar   brouwn   the
brouwn   one   kind   of   gets   stuck.

FIGURE 1–3   Beginning notebook entry of a fourth grader

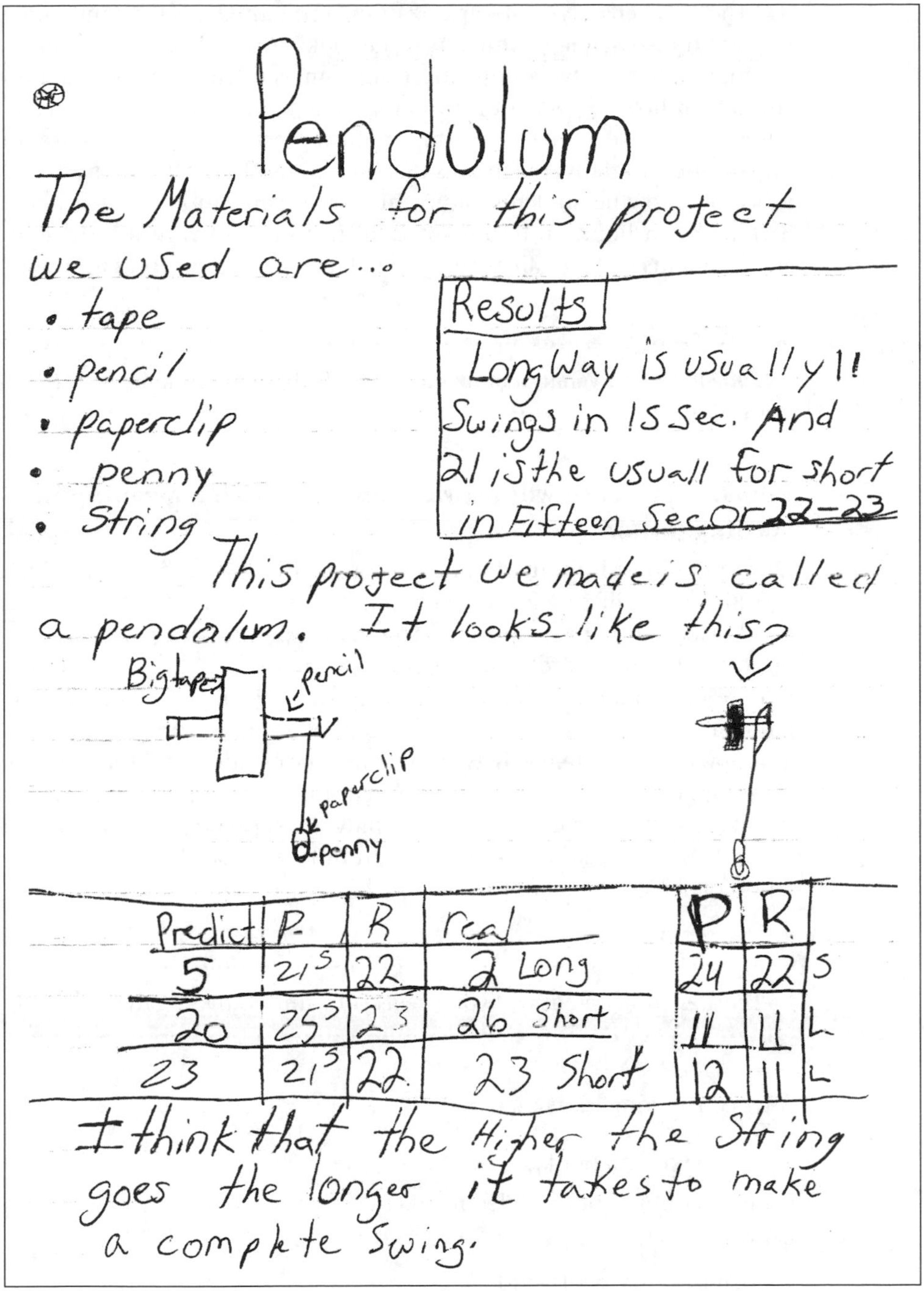

Pendulum

The Materials for this project we used are...

- tape
- pencil
- paperclip
- penny
- String

Results

Long Way is usually 11 Swings in 15 sec. And 21 is the usuall for short in Fifteen Sec. Or 22-23

This project we made is called a pendolum. It looks like this?

Big tape   pencil   paperclip   penny

Predict	P-	R	real		P	R	
5	21^5	22	2 Long		24	22	S
20	25^5	23	26 Short		11	11	L
23	21^5	22	23 Short		12	11	L

I think that the higher the string goes the longer it takes to make a complete swing.

FIGURE 1–4   Beginning notebook entry of a fifth grader

The teacher's style of organization, sequential or random, often impacts the outcome of students' notebooks. A word of caution about teaching only one style of organization: some students may have a difficult time following sequential thinking, causing frustration for both students and teacher. Yet it is important to establish some sense of organization initially; notebooks that are too random may not be useful tools. By allowing students choice in their organization, the teacher is helping them build an important skill. In time and with a little guidance, students will find an organizational technique that works for them.

Thinking point: What organizational tools do your students need?

Which experience will provide students with a meaningful starting point?

One of the most important things to consider in the beginning is which investigation will provide a solid foundation for the development of good scientific habits. The first experience should offer students the opportunity to record using various techniques. Observations that require more than one sense often work well. Having students observe familiar materials, such as fruit or the school grounds, would serve as an appropriate beginning activity. Since this investigation will set the stage for future recordings, it is important that it is engaging, promotes scientific conversation, and is developmentally appropriate. Ideas on how to set up this investigation are shared within the next section, "Implementation of Science Notebooks."

Thinking point: What will you use as your initial investigation?

After considering ideas on

- the type of notebook,
- information to be included in all entries,
- realistic expectations,
- organizational tools, and
- the initial investigation,

the teacher is ready to implement the science notebooks.

Implementation of Science Notebooks

As the teacher begins to put notebooks into practice, there are new considerations:

- What goals will science notebooks address?
- What will the first week actually look like?

What goals will science notebooks address?

One element of teaching involves setting goals for students' learning—objectives that students should achieve. In science, those goals come from state and district curricula in conjunction with the *National Science Education Standards* and the nature of science itself. The science notebooks enhance the scientific processes and encourage students to gain an understanding of scientific goals in a truly authentic manner. Content goals are often addressed in the curriculum materials adopted by districts; however, the process of science is similar across curriculum materials. Therefore, this book focuses on how science notebooks can be used in conjunction with any district curriculum and how the process goals, along with representation, help students understand the content.

With clear learning goals in mind, it is easier to facilitate students' experiences with science notebooks and guide students toward the desired understandings. Notebooks become a tool for helping students become better observers, classifiers, questioners, and so on. Notebooks may guide the teacher in planning the process skills on which to focus. For example, if students are having difficulty noting details, the teacher may focus on technical drawings to address the skill of observation. If a teacher doesn't have a clear understanding of the goals that are to be achieved, science becomes a series of activities rather than a connected investigation. The following classroom vignette demonstrates the goal setting of a teacher working with second-grade students.

At the beginning of each investigation, I look at what it is the students will be doing and consider (1) What are the content goals for this activity? For example, are students investigating the physical characteristics of an insect or determining what affects the pitch of an instrument? (2) What are the main process skills? For example, are students observing, comparing and contrasting, or collecting numerical data? In most science activities there are several process skills occurring simultaneously and it is difficult to separate them; however, I try to select one on which to focus. (3) What are different ways students might represent information?

Since I consider notebooks to be tools for the students, I focus on different ways the students might record the information, not necessarily the way I would do it. Once I have determined the focus of the lesson in terms of content, process, and representation, I am able to focus on facilitating the interactions between the students and their notebooks.

As with any good teaching, the goals of the lesson will shift according to students' needs. This book focuses on the needs of students as they pertain to representation of information in words and/or pictures within notebooks. The content goals are always in mind but may be secondary to the ways students represent them.

What will the first week actually look like?

Since science notebooks may be new to students, it is important to thoroughly plan out the first few days of use. A thorough plan allows the teacher to think through all aspects and prepare for the unexpected. Although the scientific concept may differ from lesson to lesson, the process of learning to use notebooks is quite similar in all lessons. In the following example, the teacher begins by having students observe apples to provide a common experience with a familiar material. This allows students to focus on their notebooks rather than trying to make sense of the content of the investigation. The teacher then introduces a material that will be studied more in depth, as required by the curriculum guidelines.

Day One

Objective: Students will record observations of an apple.

Materials: apple, hand lenses, notebooks

Procedure (45+ minutes):

1. Introduce the lesson: discuss with students that they will be observing an apple and recording what they notice. (2 minutes)
2. Introduce notebooks as tools to help students keep track of their observations. Discuss the essential components of every entry (date and subject) with students. (5 minutes)
3. Have students observe the apple and record their findings. (10 minutes)
4. Ask students to sit on the floor and share observations of their apple with a partner. (3 minutes)
5. Ask students to share observations as a whole group using their science notebooks. Record observations on the board. (10 minutes)

6. Have students share how they recorded their information (words, sentences, pictures). Ask students to discuss the benefits of various recording methods. (5 minutes)

7. Introduce the hand lens and how to use it.

8. Provide time for students to continue observing their apples and adding to their recording. (10 minutes)

9. If time permits, students return to the floor and share their observations, if not, begin day two with sharing.

10. Let students know they may eat the apples.

Day Two

Objective: Students will record observations of plant structures. Establish patterns of discussion.

Materials: plants, notebooks

Procedure (50 minutes):

1. Gather students on the floor to read the observations they recorded on day one. Invite students to share their observations with the whole group by asking questions about the color and shape of the apples. Ask students how they know this information. (5 minutes)

2. Ask students to look at how they recorded the information in their notebooks. Have students share various methods. (5 minutes)

3. Introduce the plant(s): share with students that they will work with partners to observe and record information about their plant. (15 minutes)

4. Have students return to the floor and share their findings with a different partner. (5 minutes)

5. Ask students to share their observations with the whole group. After one student shares his observations, provide time for other students to ask questions or make comments regarding what was shared. (10 minutes)

6. After the discussion, give students time to record any additional information they would like to add to their notebooks. (5 minutes)

7. Have students return to the plants to make further observations. (5 minutes)

Day Three

Objective: Students will record observations of plant structures. Students will be introduced to relevant vocabulary. Students will discuss methods of recording.

Materials: plants, hand lenses, notebooks

Procedure (45+ minutes):

1. Ask students to sit on the floor and individually review their note-book entries from the previous day prior to discussing their observations with a new partner. (5 minutes)

2. Have individuals share observations with the whole group. Continue to provide time for questions and comments for each student. (5 minutes)

3. Discuss with students that they will be looking at the same plants as before, but this time a hand lens will be available. (2 minutes)

4. Prior to returning to the plants, ask students to think about what they are going to observe. Allow time for students to discuss ideas with others. Once they have a focus in mind, ask the students how they plan to record their observations. Have students share how they are going to record (pictures, labels, sentences, etc.). (5 minutes)

5. Have students return to the plants and make further observations. (15 minutes)

6. Ask students to return to the floor and share observations. As students share their observations, listen for the terminology they use to describe the plant structures. Direct the students' focus on the formal vocabulary by connecting their informal language to the plant terminology. (10 minutes)

7. Prior to cleaning up, provide students with time to add to their observations. Students may or may not naturally incorporate new words that were introduced during the discussion. Encourage students to use the words if they find them helpful in describing their observations. (3 minutes)

Day Four

Objective: Students will draw and label plant structures.

Materials: plants, hand lenses, notebooks, colored pencils

Procedure (52 minutes):

1. Gather students on the floor and review their recordings from the previous days. (2 minutes)

2. In groups of three or four, ask students to discuss different ways they recorded their information. As students share, ask them to explain how they recorded their information. (5 minutes)

3. After all groups have shared how they recorded their information, focus on drawings of the plants. Discuss what information might be shown in a drawing. Guide students to notice that the plant structures can be recorded quite easily using a drawing. Ask students what else

might help them record plant structures along with the drawings. Guide students to use labels along with their drawings to show the various parts of the plant. (10 minutes)

4. Before students continue with their observations, have them discuss with a partner what they might draw and label while observing their plants. (2 minutes)

5. Introduce the colored pencils as tools that they may use to more accurately record their plant observations. (2 minutes)

6. Ask students to observe their plants and record their observations. (15 minutes)

7. Have students return to the floor and share their observations with a different partner. (5 minutes)

8. Focus the whole-group discussion on how observations were recorded. Are students drawing their plants and labeling the structures? Have students share their techniques for recording with the class. (6 minutes)

9. Have students discuss with a partner how they might improve their recording the next time they look at plants. They may need some suggestions such as using correct colors, labeling the structures, or labeling only the important things rather than everything. (5 minutes)

Day Five

Objective: Compare and contrast two different plants and their structures. Students develop strategies to record information on two different objects.

Materials: colored pencils, hand lenses, notebooks, different plants

Procedure (60 minutes):

1. Have students review their previous observations. Revisit how students might improve their recording. (5 minutes)

2. Introduce the new plant. Discuss with the students that they will be looking at a new type of plant today. Students may wish to revisit the first plant to compare it with the new plant. Have students think about how they are going to record their information on two different plants. Have a few students share their recording strategies. (10 minutes)

3. Have students observe and record information about their new plant with a partner. Students may revisit the first plant and add information to their notebooks. (10 minutes)

4. Gather students on the floor to share their findings with each other. (3 minutes)

5. Ask students to share their findings with the whole group. Students will need to clarify which plant they are discussing. (10 minutes)

6. After the students have shared, have them look at their notebooks and discuss how they were able to record information about the two separate plants. Share strategies with the whole group. (5 minutes)

7. Before returning to their plants, have students think about how they will continue to record their information. Let them know that it is okay to try new ways in order to find one that works best for them. (2 minutes)

8. Have students return to their plants and make more observations. (10 minutes)

9. Ask students to return to the floor to discuss their findings. (5 minutes)

This schedule is one way to introduce science notebooks. Teachers may have to make adjustments to accommodate student readiness. As in any subject area, the teacher needs to constantly assess where students are and adjust the plan accordingly. The next section looks more closely at the role science notebooks play in informing instructional practice.

Formative Assessment

> Formative assessment refers to assessments that provide information to students and teachers that is used to improve teaching and learning. (National Research Council 2001, 25)

What role do science notebooks play in formative assessment?

As students use their notebooks, they become formative assessment tools for both the teacher and the students, serving as an aid in terms of making learning decisions. They are not used by the teacher for summative assessment, nor are they a graded product. Rather, notebooks are tools for informing the teacher if students are meeting predetermined goals or if more instruction needs to be given. Even in the beginning stages of notebook use, it is important to consider students' progress. Following are some questions the teacher may ask regarding students' science notebooks. These may be helpful in determining where students are and what next steps may be appropriate. Other sections of this book provide further information for the teacher on next steps using the information gathered.

- Do students' drawings enhance their entries?
- How often are students using drawings and how much time are they spending on them?
- How comfortable are students in using labels with their drawings?
- How do labels enhance or detract from the drawings students create?

- Is the use of color enhancing or impeding the students' drawings?
- What types of questions are students asking and recording in their notebooks?
- How much of the students' recording is fact and how much is fiction?
- What types of recording strategies are students utilizing?
- What organizational strategies would make notebooks more useful for students?
- When observing live organisms, how do students represent the behaviors and structures of the organisms?
- What evidence do students show of their thinking and understanding?
- How do students make use of their notebooks in small- and whole-group discussions?
- When do students choose to record information in their notebooks?
- When do students choose to use information in their notebooks?

What does formative assessment look like?

While collecting and reviewing notebooks is one way to assess students' progress, there are other methods that provide similar data. Two key elements in understanding how students are using their science notebooks are observing and listening. There is a great deal to be learned by sitting back and observing how students use their science notebooks. As students work, the teacher can walk around the room and use a checklist to make note of students' methods of recording, use of process skills, or understanding of content. Class discussions serve as another source for assessing what students know. Observing how students use their notebooks during a discussion may indicate the amount of information contained in the notebooks or the usefulness of recording methods.

Thinking point: How will I gather data to formatively assess my students?

Developing Science Notebooks

Now that students have begun using notebooks, how are they supported?

One of the most important roles for the teacher is to support students' use of notebooks. In order to be used in a scientific manner, notebooks need to be available during an investigation and then utilized in discussions with others. This does not occur naturally for many students and may require assistance from the teacher to become habit. In the beginning, it may seem as though a great deal of time is being invested; consider it as time spent building a solid foundation for scientific thinking.

As students work to develop science content, they work through several experiences with the materials followed by class discussions. This cycle of interaction, described in the following sections, examines the roles of the students and the teacher throughout an investigation. It is important to note that this cycle may take place over the course of several days. The vignettes throughout the following sections describe how a teacher worked with a second-grade class throughout the cycle.

- materials: exploration
- discussion: setting the stage
- materials: recording strategies
- discussion: small and whole group
- materials: content
- discussion: content
- notebooks: reflection

Materials: Exploration

Whenever students are introduced to something new, it is important that they have time to explore the materials and concepts freely. This allows them to formulate ideas without any preconceived notions. Students may or may not record during this initial exploration—that is okay.

Discussion: Setting the Stage

This second phase of the cycle allows students to share initial ideas and provides them with the support they may need for recording. This discussion takes place only after students have manipulated the materials and had some time to form their own ideas.

> Many times throughout an investigation I gather the students to a discussion area; this is an area away from their work space where we can go over directions and discuss the activity. To get students thinking about how they might record the information, I ask leading questions. For example, "How might you organize the information you are collecting about the way water flows?" They begin by sharing their thoughts with someone sitting near them before sharing with the group; this provides everyone the opportunity to share something in a nonthreatening environment. It also allows students who may not have an

> idea or be able to verbalize their idea clearly to receive help from others. Then we share our thoughts about recording as a class; the students share their ideas about recording and then I ask the group for questions they may have about the recording strategies the students shared. Before ending the discussion, I ask students to talk about what recording strategy they plan to use when they return to the materials.

After this type of discussion, students have a variety of strategies they can use to record their thinking. This builds in a certain amount of success in using notebooks and focuses their learning for the investigation.

Materials: Recording Strategies

Once students are focused on how to record, they return to the materials. While this exploration looks similar to the initial one, there are differences. This time, the teacher formatively assesses students' learning and determines the focus of the next discussion.

> I frequently walk around during the activity to observe how students are working with the content and the process. I keep their ideas of recording strategies in the back of my mind and ask myself how the students are progressing. I only interact with the students to clarify directions or redirect their attention to the activity. They need this time with the materials to continue formulating their ideas; if I jump in too quickly, I am likely to interrupt their learning. Students need time to work uninterrupted in order to fully understand their thought processes and questions, allowing them to truly internalize the science concepts. During this time, I note if students are struggling with any of the process skills, like organizing the data or labeling.

Discussion: Small and Whole Group

This discussion period becomes a pivotal point in students' recording. Based on data gathered during the last interaction with the materials and the recording strategies used, the teacher chooses a focus for discussion. Through careful questioning, the teacher guides the students to examine various techniques.

> After a brief fifteen- to twenty-minute period working with the materials, I call the students back for a discussion using their

notebooks. I begin by asking students what type of recording strategy they used. Then I ask them to focus on one particular aspect of the investigation, directing their discussion toward the concept being learned. I give them a couple of minutes to look over their notes and make additions before they share their thoughts. I ask them to discuss with a friend, using their notebooks, what they have been doing and learning and what questions they now have. Then I ask the students to share as a class, again allowing the students time to question each other.

I never skip sharing with a friend because that is the most powerful part of the activity, as oral communication builds literacy. Students feel that sharing is valuable because they are working, making progress, and sharing that progress with each other. It holds everyone in the class accountable to each other.

Occasionally, if the content is difficult, we discuss it and I provide some guidance. However, I intentionally put off most of the content discussion until students have more time with the materials. The last thing we talk about before returning to the investigation is next steps the students will take. Again, the students discuss it with each other before sharing as a class.

Materials: Content

Once students have started to use strategies for recording information, the focus changes to understanding of the content. As students continue to work with the materials, the teacher assesses their understanding and determines next steps to take in terms of instruction.

When students return to the investigation, I observe how they are recording, but this time I am more focused on the content. I interact more with the students and ask them questions such as "What are you finding? What are your thoughts? What evidence do you have to support your thinking?" Sometimes I ask why they are recording the information the way they are. I determine how the whole class is progressing. Do they need more time with this experience or do they need more experiences to understand the content?

Discussion: Content

Science notebooks are tools to aid students in understanding scientific content. Once students have had experience with the concept and have formulated initial ideas, small- and whole-group discussions take place to help students solidify conceptual understandings.

> After students have had time to focus on the content, I call them back to the floor. I provide a few minutes for them to write down any thoughts they may have but have not yet recorded, and then I ask them to share with a partner. The purpose of this discussion is to communicate their thinking. Keeping this in mind, I often begin the group discussion with a question such as "What did you discover?" Again, the students discuss this with each other before sharing ideas with the whole group. This discussion serves as an opportunity for students to examine the purpose of their work. It also serves as a time in which I can formatively assess students' content knowledge.

Notebooks: Reflection

Students benefit from writing in science, as it allows them a means to process their thinking. By giving them time to reflect on their thoughts, the teacher is asking them to make sense of their learning. These reflections can serve as a window into their true understandings.

> Students finish recording while I walk around the room and encourage them to record any thoughts, explanations, questions, and so on that might help them later. I have found that the students who were actively engaged with the materials benefit from this time; it allows them time to process their thoughts without distractions. There were times when we were at the end of the day and students would be so engaged in recording their thoughts that they stayed even after the bell rang.

By allowing students time to work without interruptions, the teacher is helping them internalize the science concepts and make them their own. Students need time to explore their own thought processes and questions. It is the teacher's responsibility to pull the students' thoughts together and begin to help students make connections between their thoughts and the concept being explored. These connections begin to form when students share in small- and whole-group discussions.

What types of modeling support the development of science notebooks?

While students need models of science notebooks, it is important to think about how much modeling should take place. Looking first at what students are able to do independently allows the teacher to determine how much guidance to provide. To develop a repertoire of strategies, students may find it helpful to see models of various methods. Students are less likely to become dependent upon teacher guidance when they are encouraged to share their work with one another rather than learning from teacher-generated models. This allows the teacher to focus first on what students know and what they can learn from each other. If there is a particular strategy that would be beneficial, based upon the data collected through formative assessment, and students are not utilizing it, then it is important for the teacher to introduce that strategy to the students.

Thinking point: To what extent is modeling appropriate for your students?

Creating a Purpose for Notebooks

Why create a purpose?

Notebooks are an important component of scientists' work, and they should be important components of students' investigations. If students do not have a purpose for them, notebooks simply become a busy activity. Students also need a reason to record while they work; otherwise the materials are too alluring and recording does not take place. Students gain a better appreciation of the notebooks' value if they use them in an authentic manner.

How is an authentic purpose for science notebooks created?

Scientists use their notebooks on a daily basis in the work they do and in conversations with others, similar to the way students use their notebooks. By having students use science notebooks to create a presentation of scientific findings to share with a larger audience, the teacher establishes an authentic purpose. Teachers should encourage students to share their understandings in scientific presentations to others that can be summatively assessed. These scientific presentations might take the form of an oral sharing, an expository text, a report, a slide show presentation, or a poster. Students use their notebooks to reference their questions, procedures, results, conclusions, and any new questions they may have while creating their presentations. The following vignette shows how fifth graders shared their understandings of environments.

My class had been studying different types of environments and how changes would impact plant growth. My scientific content goal was for students to recognize that several environmental factors influence plant growth. Groups of students had planned and begun working on investigations based on questions they generated. A few days into their work, I announced that they would be sharing their investigations and results in the form of a slide show using a familiar computer program. The notebooks served as tools for students to recall their plans, data, thinking, results, and questions as they began to work on their slide shows. Students who recorded a great deal in their notebooks found them very helpful, while those who did not relied upon others. Following the presentations of their investigations, there was a noticeable change in students' recordings.

What is the vision for science notebooks?

The teacher's understanding of what is to be accomplished with science notebooks is used to create a vision of what the notebooks will look like and how they will be used. Naturally, this vision will evolve over time. The following vignette examines one teacher's vision over the first three years of notebook use.

Notebook development for me went from being very structured and teacher-centered to very student-centered over the course of three years. In my first year of implementing notebooks, my goal was student mastery of recording strategies. I wanted to show them all the different recording strategies I knew. I set up the structure for them, told them what to record, and showed them how to record it. Most of the notebooks looked similar, and many students met the goals. Reflecting back, I wonder if students really understood the strategies they used or if they were just following my directions.

The following year, I wanted my students to take more ownership of their notebooks. My goal was for students to select appropriate recording techniques. I introduced them to various recording strategies but left the decisions of what and how to record up to the students. When I looked at their notebooks, I focused on when and how they used the strategies. Over the course of the year, I began to realize that my students were using strategies I introduced to them, but they were not utilizing any other strategies. As students represented their understanding of the content, they used various recording strategies, but the data represented looked similar. At the end of the year, I wondered if the students really understood those strategies or if they used them only because they thought that was the expectation.

In the third year, I gave control of the notebooks over to the students. My goal was for students to use notebooks in a way that made sense to them. At the beginning of the year, students brainstormed ideas for recording strategies, which were posted in the room for reference throughout the year. My mantra for the year became "Record in a way that will make sense to you later." As the year progressed, I provided time for students to share the new strategies they were developing. I decided that the notebooks belonged to the students, not me, and stopped looking in them. Instead, I used conversations and presentations as guides in making my teaching decisions. I listened carefully to see what data and explanations they provided and evidence of their learning of scientific ideas to inform the choices I made.

Thinking point: What benefits and limitations are there to various amounts of structure?

There are many things to take into consideration when implementing science notebooks in the classroom. This chapter has brought those factors to light and posed thinking points throughout. Following are two final thinking points that are crucial to successful implementation of science notebooks.

Thinking point: Where are your students starting? What do you expect to accomplish with science notebooks?

Elements of a Science Notebook

Recording and Organizing Data

What does recording and organizing data look like?

In science, the need arises for students to record and organize the information they are gathering. Whether it is observing the weather or measuring plant growth, there is a variety of data involved in student investigations. In working with this data, there is a wide array of recording and organizational methods available to students. Some of those methods are

- notes and lists,
- technical drawings and diagrams with labels,
- charts,
- tables,
- graphs, and
- written observations.

The most common methods are probably lists or quick notes that students record in their notebooks in order to capture the work they are doing. It is important for teachers to remember that these are the students' notes and they should not be subjected to the same criteria put upon other student writing. In real-world note taking, capitalization, punctuation, and grammar are not the focus, the content is; however, notes must be taken in a manner that makes sense. With this in mind, it is reasonable for teachers to expect students to make sense of their notes as well.

> *Thinking point:* What organizational expectations will you have for your students as they record? How will your expectations change over time?

Figures 2–1 through 2–3 demonstrate three different ways students recorded and organized the same data.

How do students begin recording and organizing data?

Like scientists, it is important that students become comfortable recording during the science investigation—recording their observations and data while they work in order to reference the information later as they organize and analyze their results. To accomplish this, it is important that notebooks be available during an investigation. This means notebooks may get dirty, wrinkled, and wet; however, this creates the ability to record important information as it is being learned.

When students are first introduced to a material or to science notebooks, they may find it difficult to focus on recording. Therefore, it is important for teachers to provide students with time to experience and explore the material and then encourage recording. The following vignette examines the method one teacher used to introduce notebooks to his second-grade students.

Getting my second graders to record data was something that I knew was going to be a pretty hefty time investment; however, it was one that I considered to be worthwhile. It seemed that there were two ways to approach this task: (1) I could focus on the students and allow their ideas to guide the lesson or (2) I could build the lesson around my ideas and hope the students understood the concept. I decided I would place the focus on the students by watching their actions, listening to their conversations and questions, noticing what they chose to record, and helping them make sense of it.

On the first day of school, my class and I investigated insects, an area typically of interest for the students as well as myself. Before we started looking at the mealworm larva, I introduced the notebooks and set my expectations: students needed to record the date and any information they felt was important. I did not set requirements for recording; their instructions were to record anything they found important. Upon receiving the mealworms, their interest shifted from the notebooks to the mealworm; this I expected. I walked around, listening and discussing with them what they were seeing. They were all actively engaged in observing the mealworms. However, very few recorded their observations. I made a mental note at that time to provide them with time to record.

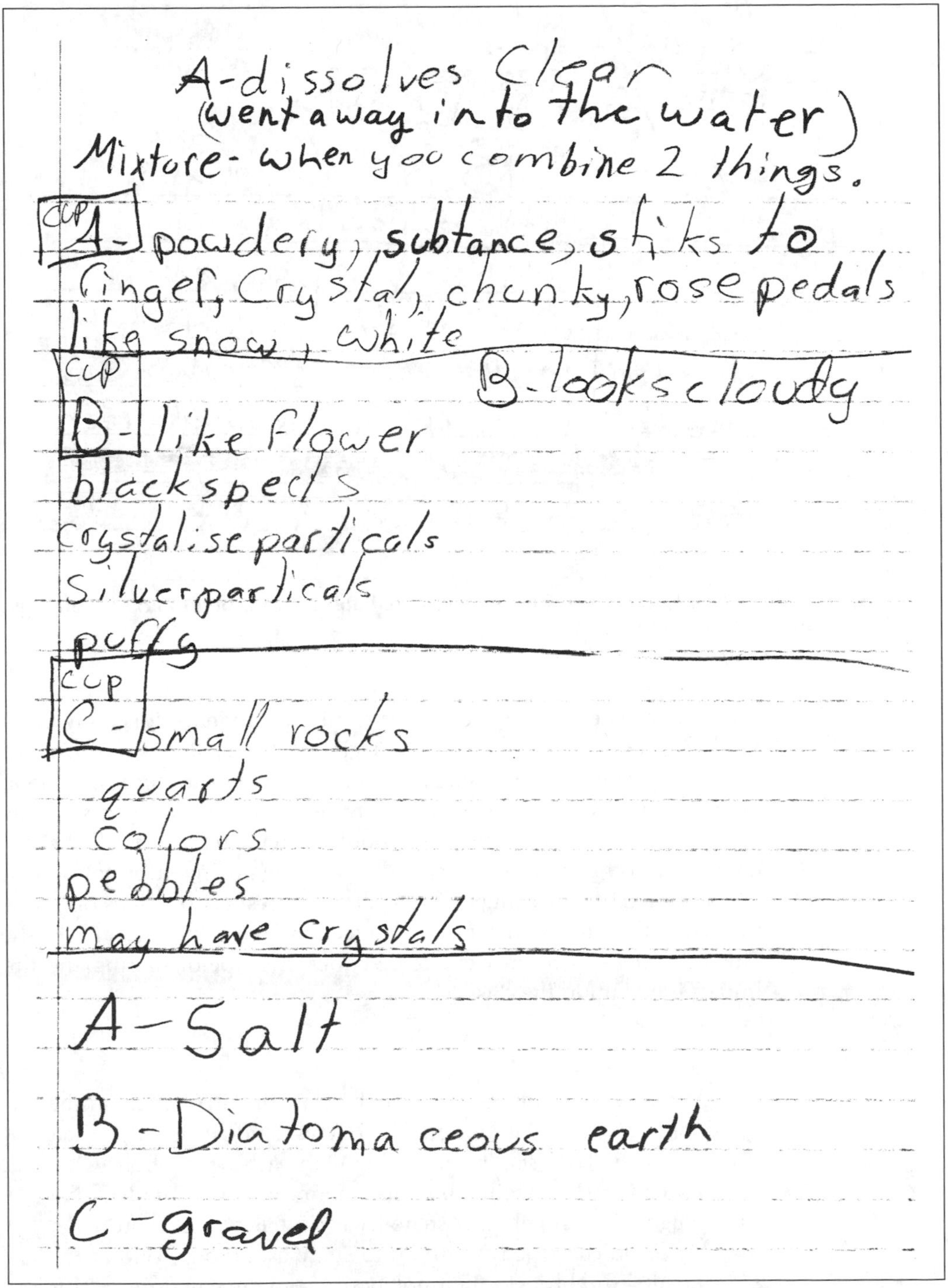

A-dissolves (clear
(went away into the water)
Mixture- when you combine 2 things.
[CUP] A- powdery, subtance, stiks to
finger, crystal, chunky, rose pedals
like snow, white

[CUP]   B- looks cloudy
B- like flower
black specks
crystalise particals
silver particals
puffs

[CUP]
C- small rocks
quarts
colors
pebbles
may have crystals

A- Salt

B- Diatomaceous earth

C- gravel

FIGURE 2–1   Three fifth-grade students represented observations on unknown materials in unique ways (see Figures 2–2 and 2–3).

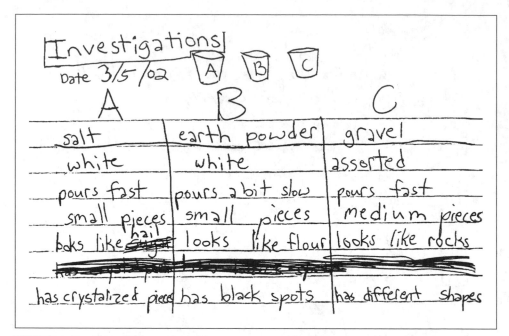

FIGURE 2–2   Three fifth-grade students represented observations on unknown materials in unique ways (see Figures 2–1 and 2–3).

While new materials may pose a distraction to students, for many notebooks are new and students may struggle with ideas of how and what to record. Students can be excellent resources for one another in this area. One way of exposing students to recording methods is to have students talk with a partner using their notebooks as references. This allows students to see other methods of recording and organizing information in a very informal way. Inviting different students to share provides opportunities for others to see that a variety of techniques can be used effectively. The following classroom vignette describes this type of sharing and the impact it had upon the class.

After looking at the mealworms, the class met in a circle on the floor to discuss what they observed. A few students brought their notebooks. They started by talking with each other about what they had noticed while observing the mealworms. The few that brought their notebooks shared with a fellow classmate what they recorded. When we began to share as a group, one of the students who brought their notebooks read directly from it. This sharing probably served as a stimulus for many of my students

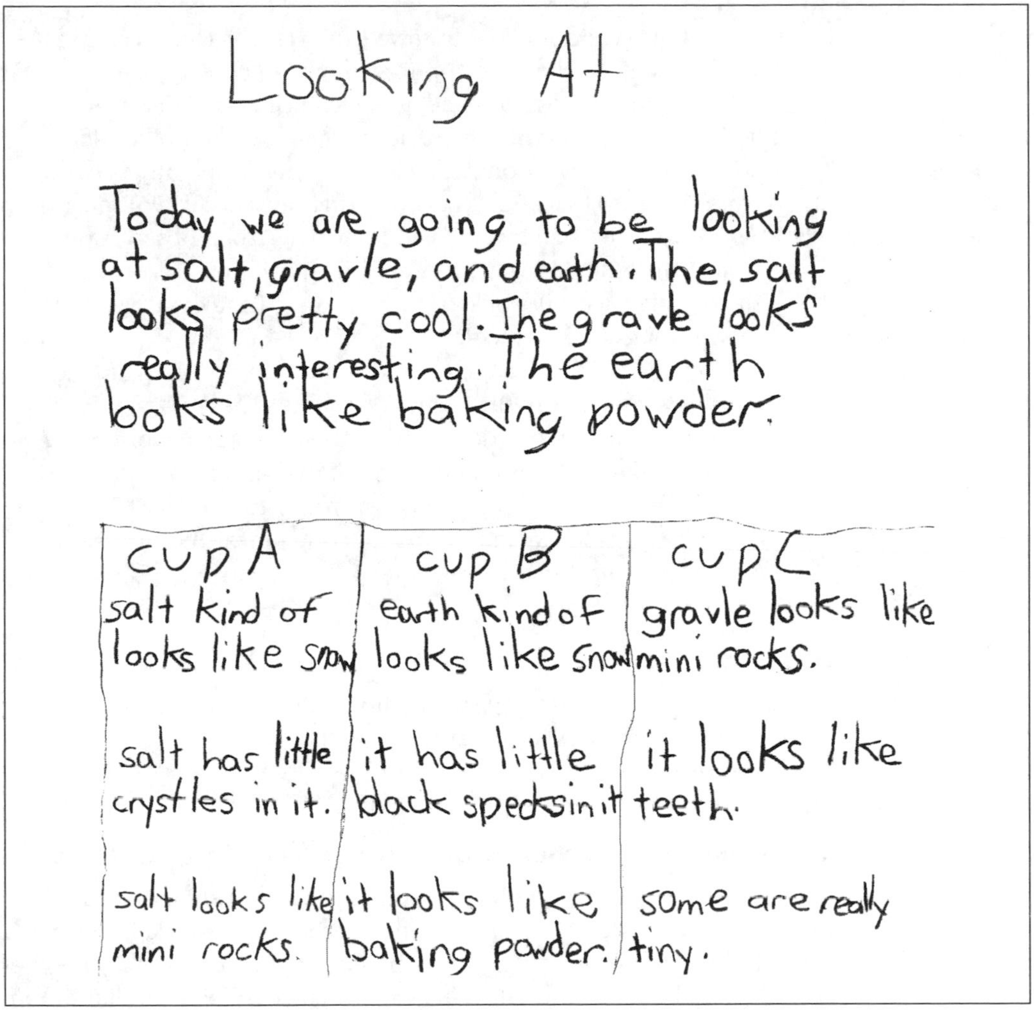

Looking At

Today we are going to be looking
at salt, gravle, and earth. The salt
looks pretty cool. The gravle looks
really interesting. The earth
looks like baking powder.

cup A	cup B	cup C
salt kind of looks like snow	earth kind of looks like snow	gravle looks like mini rocks.
salt has little crystles in it.	it has little black specks in it	it looks like teeth.
salt looks like mini rocks.	it looks like baking powder.	some are really tiny.

FIGURE 2–3 Three fifth-grade students represented observations on unknown materials in unique ways (see Figures 2–1 and 2–2).

who had not recorded anything. I remember hearing one girl say, "Oh, I should have written that down."

As we finished our first day with the mealworms, I began to think about what may have prevented my students from writing in their notebooks.

• Did they have enough time to write?
• Did they know how to write in this context?
• Did they know what to write?

On the second day, we followed the same cycle of observation, followed by sharing. I noticed more notebooks being utilized to record observations and as a reference during discussions. I noticed, during partner discussions, that a couple of students recorded their observations using a list format, while others drew pictures. During the whole-group sharing, I asked for volunteers to show how they had recorded and organized their observations. As students shared, others observed how they recorded. I responded to each student by simply saying, "Thank you for sharing," avoiding any judgments.

Over the next few days, I noticed more and more students recording observations in their notebooks. The students who had trouble writing recorded with pictures. I began a word bank for commonly used words and placed it in the front of the room for students to refer to when they wrote. By the end of the first week, most students had recorded some information about their mealworms. My role was to take them further.

Thinking point: How do your instructional decisions impact what your students view as important?

When does the teacher actually teach recording strategies?

Getting students to record observations is the initial step; helping them expand upon the depth of their recording is the larger task. To take students beyond the initial stage, it will be important to model a variety of recording and organizational strategies. Students serve as excellent models for one another for methods with which they may have experience; however, additional methods can be provided through teacher modeling. This modeling provides students with resources to draw upon during future investigations. The minilesson, a short ten-minute lesson structured around a recording method that would be appropriate to use with the investigation, is useful here. An organizational tool, such as a table or chart, can be introduced to students by collecting class results and organizing them on the board. For example, while investigating properties of liquids, students recognize the need for an organizational tool. The teacher may choose to introduce a new strategy such as a chart in order to compare the properties of each liquid. After compiling data as a class, the teacher introduces the chart as one way to organize the data. Next, the teacher provides a skeleton of a chart, allowing students to determine the heading for each category. Once headings are in place, the teacher may model one or two examples of data entry before providing time for students to complete the chart with guidance.

What about the materials provided in the adopted program?

Still another way to share recording methods with students is to access resources available in an adopted program. Some programs provide student sheets to go along with activities; some of these sheets introduce students to new methods for organizing their data. Teachers may utilize these sheets rather than having students reconstruct a chart or table in their notebooks. Students use the sheets to record their data and insert them by folding the sheet in half and stapling it into their science notebooks. Some teachers reduce these sheets on the copier so students can paste them on the pages of their notebooks. Others have made overheads of student sheets to provide those in need of a starting point an idea of one way to organize information without limiting their recording.

Technical Drawings

Technical drawings are "text elements that communicate meaning; they refine, clarify, and extend" student entries (Moline 1995, 16).

What are technical drawings?

Students are so accustomed to writing, often narrative text, that they do not think of drawing as a way to communicate their understandings. One method of recording that is often overlooked by both teachers and students is the technical drawing. Technical drawings are a powerful way to record observations and share information with others; they include more attention to detail than typical drawings. In order to draw something well, individuals must observe it closely, noting every small feature and fine line; capturing this type of detail in technical drawings enhances observation skills. The next three vignettes share a second-grade teacher's experience with technical drawings.

> While working with insects my students had spent some time observing waxworms. However, some of them were experiencing difficulty recording their observations for different reasons; some of them, being ESL learners or beginning writers, were limited in the words they had available to them. I realized my students were in need of another tool they could use to record their observations with more detail. We began to explore various drawing techniques.

What is the first step?

Many teachers believe they are not artists and do not feel they can use technical drawings to record their own observations, let alone help their students record observations with technical drawings. When drawing, many people use symbols, such as stick people or the circle flower, to represent an object rather than closely observing that object and drawing exactly what they see. Figures 2–4 and 2–5 show the difference between a symbol and a technical drawing. However, with a little practice and guidance, everyone can experience success with technical drawings and go beyond recording a symbol to recording a detailed drawing.

In order to help students be successful with technical drawings, teachers need to offer them support. A guided drawing is a process in which the teacher and students look at an object together and discuss what they see. The teacher draws the object on the board and encourages students to draw along on their own papers. At this beginning point, many of the drawings will look similar; this is fine. Through guided drawings students are gaining experience with the tools of drawing as well as realizing the observational skills needed to draw an object accurately. This initial support is crucial. If teachers simply ask students to draw technically without providing them with the tools, the outcome will be frustration for both the teacher and the students.

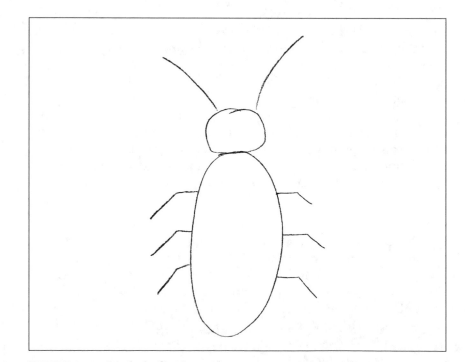

FIGURE 2–4   Symbol of an insect

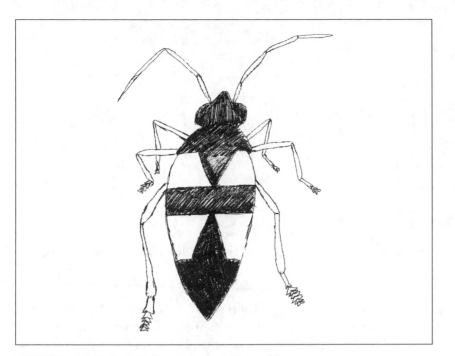

FIGURE 2–5   Technical drawing of a milkweed bug

To begin guided drawings, the teacher and the students look closely at the object that is to be drawn. They notice how parts of the object (a head, a wing, etc.) resemble basic shapes (square, rectangle, circle, oval, triangle, rhombus). They examine the entire object, noting the various shapes that are present, and choose the largest or main shape of the object and draw that on the paper. Once it is down on the paper, the teacher and students soften the sides or reconfigure it slightly so the appearance matches that of the object more closely. They then continue to add to their drawings by using basic shapes that are modified slightly to more closely match the object. This process, or the stages of a technical drawing, is shown in Figure 2–6.

What other types of support do students need?

A support that many find helpful to use is a blackline master of the object being drawn. It is easier to see lines that have already been drawn than it is to find lines on an object. Many curricula offer drawings of the various materials with which students are working. Using a copier, the teacher enlarges these drawings, if needed, to a point that students can easily see the shapes and lines present. When using a blackline master to guide the drawing, it is important for the teacher to emphasize that this

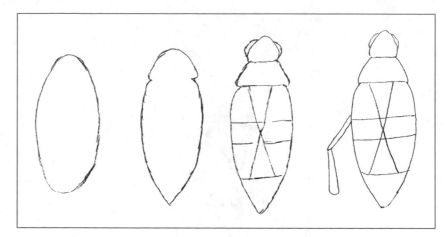

FIGURE 2–6   Beginning stages for technical drawing of a milkweed bug

is one interpretation of the way the object looks and that it is only a guide. The students must examine the original object closely, perhaps with the use of a hand lens, and add details that might be different from those included on the blackline copy.

> Through close examination of a blackline master, my students began to look at the waxworm differently. Looking for shapes allowed them to describe it more efficiently than their previous description of "round." When comparing the actual waxworm with the blackline representation, the students started to see that different parts of the waxworm were different shades and the different parts had features they had not noticed. Using hand lenses, they saw hair extending from the waxworm's body. They noticed "holes" on the sides of the waxworms. These features were then incorporated into their drawings.

Figure 2–7 shows one student's drawing from this lesson.

Proportion is another important factor to examine. In order to draw an object accurately, students need to pay attention to the proportions of the object. When drawing an insect, students look closely at the size of the head in comparison with the body. Then they examine where the legs are attached to the body. Teachers can ask questions to focus students and help them to record their observations more accurately. For example: "Are there markings on the body that would help in placing the legs? How far apart are the legs? Where does one leg end in relationship to another?"

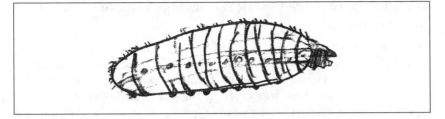

FIGURE 2–7   A second grader's technical drawing of a waxworm

Thinking point: What opportunities within your curriculum allow students to use technical drawings?

Once students understand the techniques of technical drawings, it is important that the teacher builds in opportunities for practice. Many students find it easy to communicate with drawings, but those who may still not consider themselves artists may forgo technical drawings unless encouraged to include them in their notebooks. Later, when students are comfortable with drawing, they will begin to freely include technical drawings in their notebook entries. They will use the tools mentioned earlier (proportion, shapes, blackline masters) to create original drawings. As teachers, it is important to be patient and understand that completing technical drawings is worth the time they take. It is important that students be provided with the time to record their observations by drawing and that they are sometimes asked to represent their thinking using drawings.

Although some students (as well as myself) could not draw very well, I noticed that looking at the details and attempting to re-create them on paper brought forth new ideas and concepts, such as spiracles. Throughout the year, my students had many opportunities to draw many different things. Often they asked if they could draw the details like they did with the waxworms. They did not always include such details, but when they had the time, they did. They noticed more and more details and recorded more and more details, not just with words, but also with drawings.

Thinking point: How do technical drawings fit in with how you teach science?

What other ways are technical drawings used to enhance understanding?

Technical drawings provide a wealth of information to the readers. Drawings can be enhanced through the use of labels. "Labeled diagrams work like glossaries and they can be a more powerful tool than vocabulary lists . . . the words are supported by the pictures which help to define or explain the meanings of the words especially for very young students or those students who are learning English as a second language" (Moline 1995, 23). By asking students to draw and label an object rather than label a worksheet, teachers gain a better idea of the students' understanding and of what they are able to do independently. The components students include in their drawings, or those components they leave out, provide the teacher with a window into what children see as important. Creating their own drawings with labels is by far more challenging and worthwhile than labeling existing diagrams and allows students to utilize informal terms or formal vocabulary.

Students' Questions

> When we interact with the materials, there are inherent questions in our actions with those materials. (Dyasi 2002)

What are students' questions?

In science, students raise different types of questions; some questions are about directions or procedures, while others capture a curiosity—a need to know why something is the way it is. Questioning takes place between students as well as between the students and the teacher. There are also times when the questions students ask are never spoken nor documented in writing. Obviously, some students' questions lend themselves to science investigation more than others. As teachers of science, it is important to capitalize on this curiosity and students' natural questions, bringing awareness to questions that can be investigated and working with students to recognize and record them.

What can be done to help students recognize their questions?

Often, students don't recognize that they have a question they are exploring; rather, they see it simply as an attempt to determine how something works. When students are manipulating materials, the teacher can help students recognize the questions they are asking. By talking with them, the teacher can discover what their students are thinking and help them reword their thoughts as questions. The following vignette describes how a fifth-grade teacher guided a group of students to recognize their questions.

> As my students were exploring pendulums, I noticed a group that was changing the height from which the pendulum was dropped. I went over to their table and asked them what they were investigating. The students responded, "We want to see if it will swing longer if we drop it from up here" (indicating a higher location than the original starting point).
>
> "Oh, so you want to see how changing the starting position affects the length of time the pendulum swings?" By rephrasing the question in this way, I changed it from a yes or no question to an open-ended question.

How do I help students record questions that are worthy of investigation?

Once students begin to ask their own questions, the teacher should model the importance of capturing these questions for future reference. A class "research board" serves as a place to capture students' questions. During the early stages of forming questions, students often create queries that can be answered with yes or no. It is important to call their attention to this and begin to work at rephrasing these questions in order to make them more open-ended because open-ended questions allow thinking to be extended beyond the initial question. If a child asks, "Do turtles like lettuce?" the teacher may rephrase it as "What food does the turtle prefer?"

As students become comfortable asking open-ended questions, they then begin to explore the difference between questions for investigation and research questions. One way to do this is to have the students record their questions on sentence strips. The teacher then categorizes the questions with the class according to those that can be answered by further work with the materials versus those that require consulting an expert (book, person, Internet, etc.). Once students have an idea of the two categories, they can continue to sort their questions. It is important for students to understand the difference between the two types of questions in order for them to continue to investigate independently. The following vignette shares how a teacher worked with third-grade students to sort their questions.

> After providing students with opportunities to develop questions, the teacher asked them to share their questions with one

or two of their peers. This sharing time allowed students to hear what others were exploring while exposing them to various questioning styles. As other students' questions sparked their interest, students began recording them in their own notebooks. The teacher then asked students to select two or three questions from their notebooks to record on sentence strips, which they hung around the room. Together they sorted the questions into the teacher-selected categories of "can be answered by working with the materials," "must be answered by an expert or book," and "not sure." The teacher and the students reworded those questions that were placed in the "not sure" category and then added them to one of the two other columns. At this point, students had created questions they could investigate.

Thinking point: What are reasonable expectations for your students in terms of developing and recording questions that can be investigated?

What do students do with their questions once they are recorded?

Questions are the heart of a scientific investigation. The investigation may actually begin with a teacher- or program-generated question, but it is the students' questions that fuel their desire to know more and do more with their investigations. Students may come to the end of an investigation to find that they are only just beginning and that the work they have done has actually generated more questions than it answered. By keeping those questions in their notebooks, students are able to refer back to them during future investigations, as scientists do. Figure 2–8 shows how one student recorded questions within the notebook.

The following vignette explains a teacher's thinking on the importance of students' questions.

One of the biggest motivators for my students in recording questions was the opportunity to investigate their own questions. After the first investigation based upon their own questions, students began recording more questions in hopes of being able to investigate them.

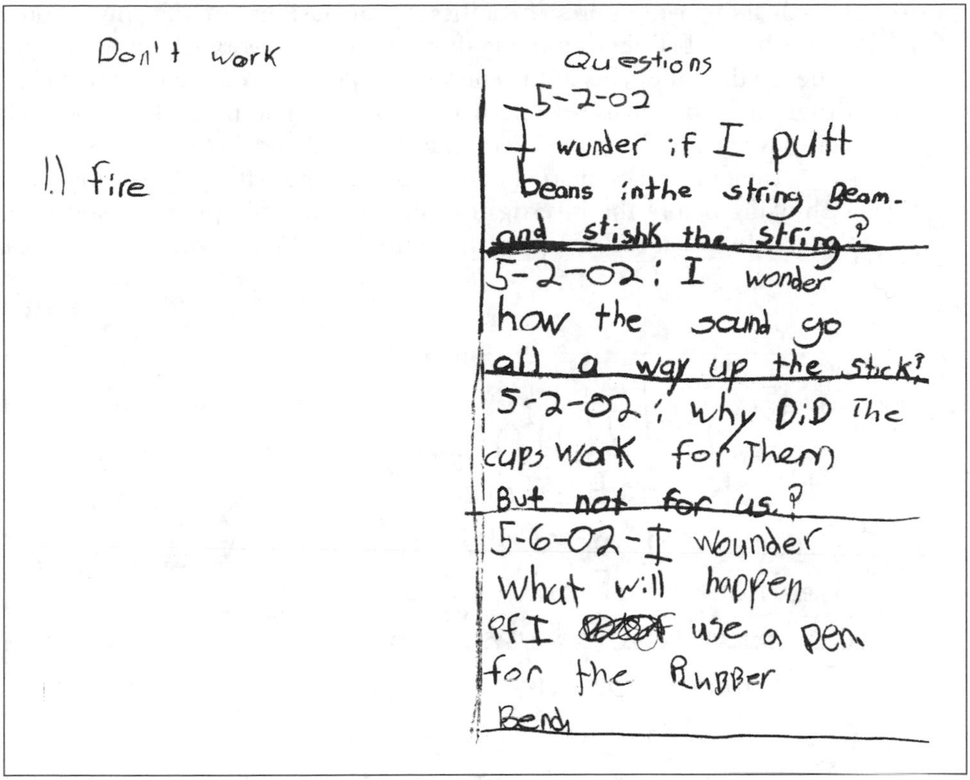

Don't work

1.) fire

Questions

5-2-02
I wunder if I putt beans inthe string Beam. and stishK the string?

5-2-02: I wonder how the sound go all a way up the stick?

5-2-02: why DiD The cups work for Them But not for us?

5-6-02-I wounder what will happen ifI use a pen for the Rubber Bend

FIGURE 2–8 A sample of recorded questions in a fourth grader's notebook

Recording Thinking

What does it mean to record thinking?

As students work in science, they are gathering data that is essential to their work. At some point, it is important that they attempt to make sense of their data, to examine what it means, why their results may differ from others, and how they plan to proceed. By asking students to record their thinking, teachers are asking them to do much more than simply reflect on the activity—they are asking their students to reflect on their thought processes and how they came to their way of thinking, to use data collected as evidence to support or change ideas about concepts, and to share questions they now have.

What does it look like when students record their thinking?

While some students may record their thoughts using complete sentences, most will use fragments. Students' thinking may be recorded as predictions, conjectures, hypotheses, conclusions, or drawings. Some students embed their thinking throughout their work while others synthesize their thoughts at the end. It is important to remember that children are individuals and need to record their thinking in a way that makes sense to them, as shown in Figures 2–9 and 2–10.

Thinking takes place before, during, and after an investigation. Thinking before the investigation involves planning the investigation, predicting what may happen, and connecting ideas to prior experiences.

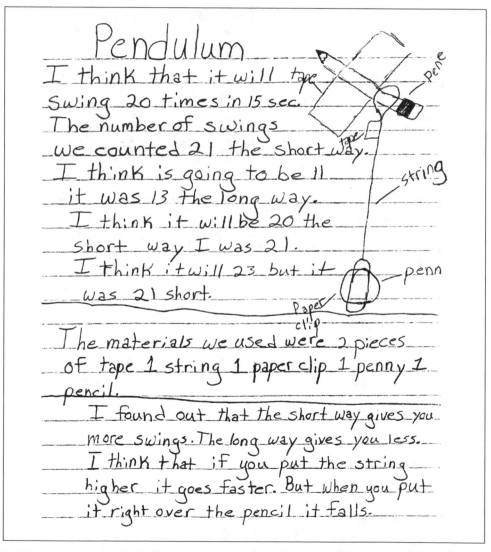

FIGURE 2–9   A record of a fifth grader's thinking while working with pendulums for the first time

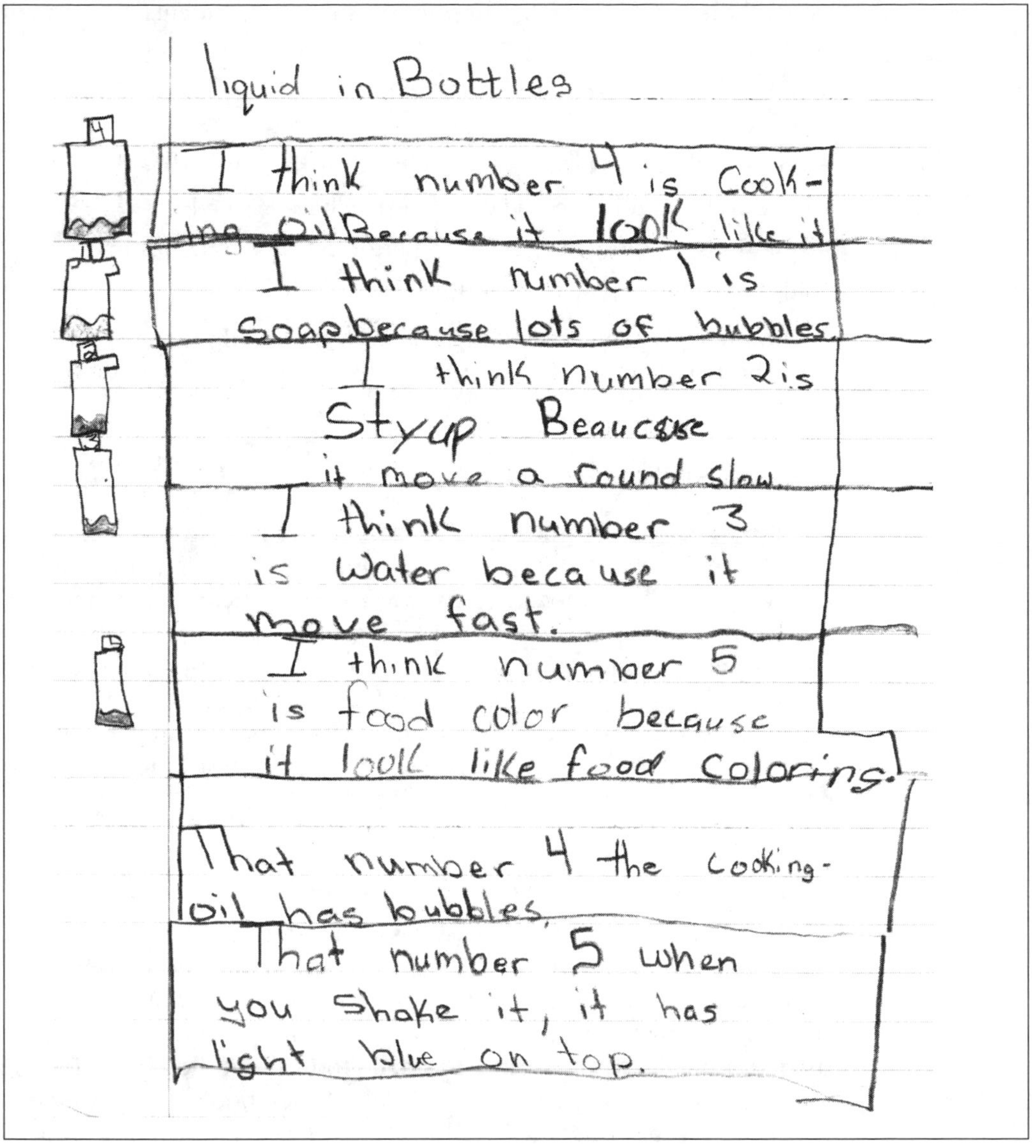

FIGURE 2–10 A fourth grader's record of thinking while working with bottles of various liquids

Considering outcomes before the investigation guides students to look for evidence that will prove or disprove their thinking during their work. How students record their thinking during the investigation differs from how they record observations; students have to not only communicate what they are observing but interpret that information and process it. Initially, this may be difficult for the students; however, with time and practice they will improve. After the investigation, students record their thinking as

- reflections on what they noticed and how that may impact future investigations;
- concrete thoughts based on the evidence gathered;
- new understandings based on what they have learned;
- questions resulting from the recognition of gaps in their thinking; or
- ideas of what they will try next.

The following vignette describes how two fourth-grade students explored their thoughts.

> The summer school extension academy began at 8:30 each morning during the last three weeks of June. About a week into the academy, one student started arriving at 8:15 each morning. He would take out his notebook and begin to independently write. As other students started to arrive and look at their materials from the previous day, he would continue to write, reflecting on his experiences from the prior day and recording his gathered thoughts about where he would begin that day. During the final week, a second student joined in this morning ritual. Together, they would sit and share their notebooks, discussing and recording their thoughts.

How do students record their thinking?

Recording thinking is not an easy task for students; many understand what is happening but struggle when it comes to translating their thoughts into words. Figure 2–11 shows a student's attempt at recording thinking. One way to support students is to provide them with time to discuss and write with a partner or small group about their ideas. During these discussions, they examine each other's notebooks and gather evidence of how they might record their thinking in their own notebooks.

In this vignette the teacher explains how second graders worked in groups as they explained their thinking.

> After discussing their observations on air in containers, I asked the students to share their thoughts on what they observed. After ten minutes of sharing, the students recorded their thoughts on why they believed the air acted the way it did. Their writing contained hypotheses that were supported by their observations.

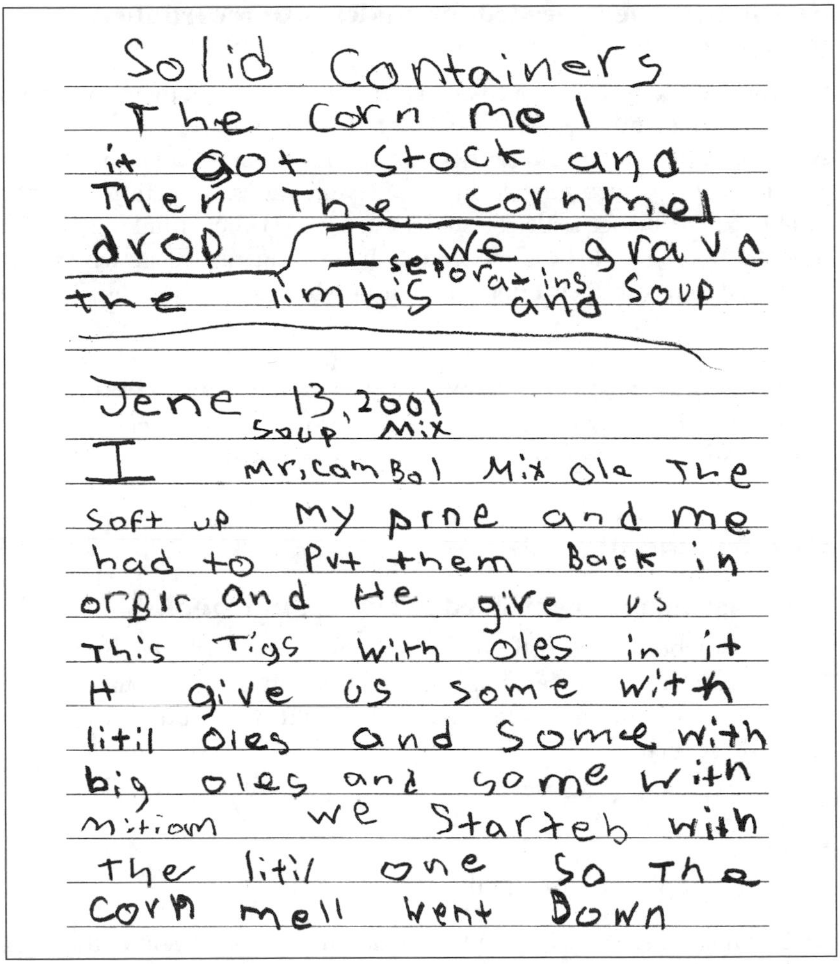

FIGURE 2–11   A fourth grader's initial attempt at recording thinking demonstrates action and some thought.

As they wrote, the students shared their thoughts in small groups. Students found this sharing time beneficial, especially if they had difficulty putting their thoughts into words. Over time, more and more students began sharing and recording their thinking on their own. I started to hear my students say, "Hold on, I just had a thought. I need to write it down before I forget it," or "What she said reminded me of something I was thinking." Students started to link their new thoughts to prior thoughts as well as other students' thinking—very similar to what scientists do.

How much time is needed for students to record their thinking?

Students should be encouraged and given time to write in their notebooks before, during, and after an investigation. Students cannot be expected to synthesize their thinking in thirty seconds; time must be built into the lesson. How this is incorporated into the lesson varies. Sometimes specific time needs to be set aside for students to record their thinking, and at other times it needs to be embedded in the investigation. If students don't have time to record their thinking, their notebooks may become just logs of data.

> *Thinking point:* How and when will you provide time to reflect?

Other Elements

What else might be included in science notebooks?

Science notebooks are collections of information gathered over time. There are some basic elements of notebooks that help document the process students are going through and should be included with every entry. These include

- date
- time
- heading (topic, title, or question)

Each of these elements aids students when they look back at entries and analyze their data; therefore, it is a good idea to establish the habit of including these elements with every entry.

There are other elements that are not essential to science notebooks; however, they may be powerful tools for the students to use from time to time. When working with materials students may find it helpful to collect samples, when appropriate, and include them in their entries. A leaf sample, insect molt, or results from a chromatography experiment may be taped in for future reference. When a sample is not a viable option, students may want to consider including a rubbing of the object in order to capture the texture of it.

There are times when neither a sample nor a rubbing is possible, and a drawing would be too difficult. In these situations a photo might capture the event (digital cameras allow for immediate viewing). Students like to include photos in their notebooks, so it is important for teachers to think carefully about the use of this technology. For some items drawings may be more appropriate than photos, as drawings require close observation and attention to detail. For more information on drawing, please refer to the section "Technical Drawings" on page 31.

Photos can also be used to capture those moments when students are so engaged with the materials that recording in their notebooks would be difficult. The photos can be inserted into their science notebooks, and students can use them as prompts to write about the experience. This type of writing is called photojournalism and is a motivating tool for students. Figure 2–12 shows a sample of photojournalism.

We felt so happy about what we did! We banged the tuning fork on the wood block and put the tuning fork next to the ping pong ball and it bounces! Because it was new! We used a tuning fork, a wood block and a ping pong ball. The ping pong ball is touched by the vibrating tuning fork. We know that the tuning fork is viberating by feeling it move and seeing it move.

FIGURE 2–12   Sample of photojournalism

It is important that students are able to recall the materials they worked with in an experiment; however, students do not always need to write a materials list. Quite often students include the materials they used within the explanation of what they did or within drawings and the reader needs only to extract that information, as shown in Figure 2–13.

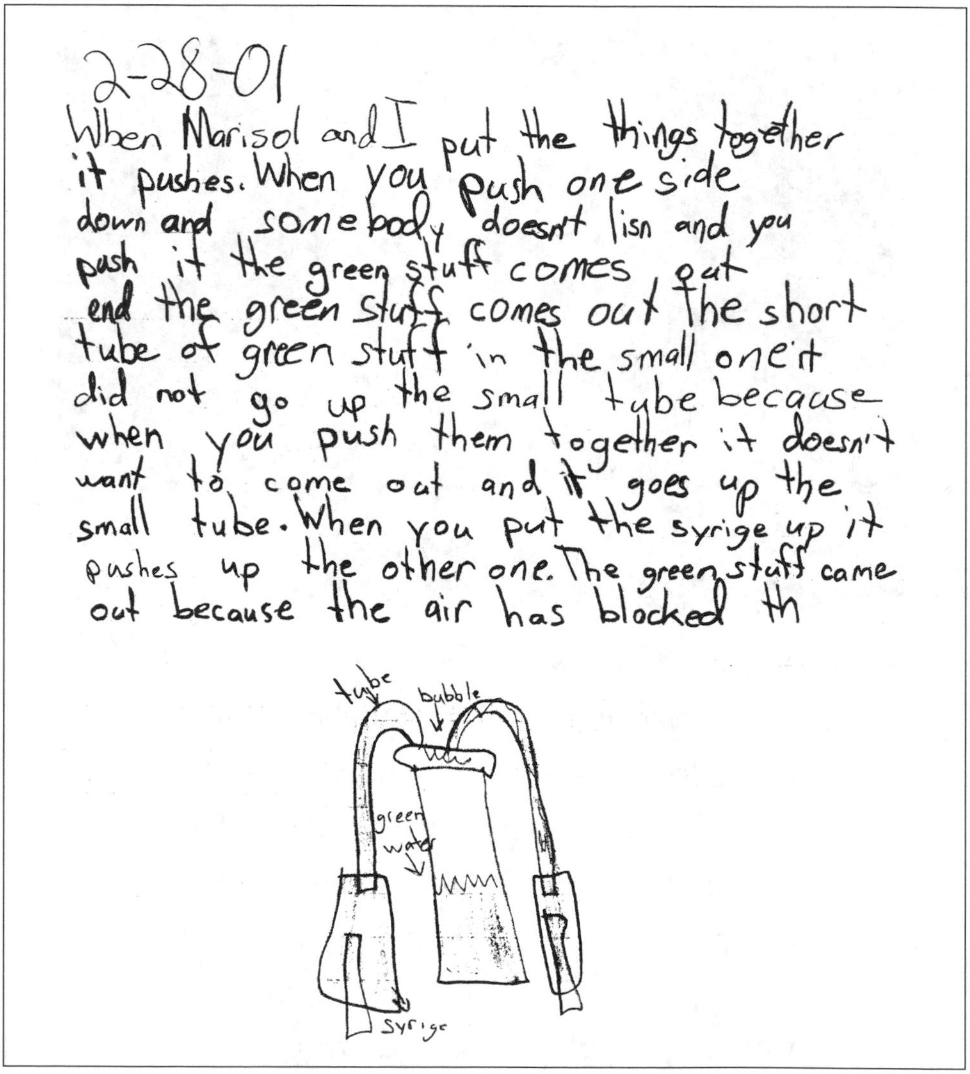

2-28-01

When Marisol and I put the things together it pushes. When you push one side down and somebody doesn't lisn and you push it the green stuff comes out end the green stuff comes out the short tube of green stuff in the small one it did not go up the small tube because when you push them together it doesn't want to come out and it goes up the small tube. When you put the syrige up it pushes up the other one. The green stuff came out because the air has blocked th

tube   bubble

green water

syrige

FIGURE 2–13   A second-grade student embeds the materials used while drawing and writing about the investigation.

Elementary teachers are always looking for ways to integrate curricula and many teachers have pulled various features of expository text into science notebooks. These include the table of contents, glossary, and index. If teachers choose to incorporate these features, they need to consider how they will be utilized and if the time spent setting them up will be worthwhile. Chapter 6, "Literacy Connections," offers information on using science notebooks as a context for literacy development.

Thinking point: How will students make use of expository text features (glossary, index, etc.) in future lessons?

3

Signs of Student Progress

Science notebooks are meant to be tools for students, utilized during science investigations and discussions as records of information and resources in conversations. Students capture data, drawings, questions, and reflections in their notebooks. They reference them during group discussions to synthesize their ideas. As students gain experience with utilizing notebooks, their abilities within each of these areas progress. Students routinely assess their work and set goals for themselves as learners. This chapter examines how students progress in utilizing notebooks from beginning to more advanced stages of use.

Predicting

What evidence of progress is there in students' predictions?

> Prediction is the use of knowledge to identify and explain observations, or changes, in advance. (National Research Council 1996, 116)

Too often, students equate making a prediction with guessing; they attempt to decide an outcome without the benefit of any experiences on which to base the decision. For this reason, students' predictions may begin as nothing more than random guessing. Their predictions may make little sense in the scheme of their notebooks. Without the fundamental understanding of predictions, students sometimes become frustrated when confronted with data that does not match their prediction. At this stage, students often want their predictions to be correct, so they look for indications of this and end up reading more into the data or manipulating it to make it match their ideas. Other students may actually alter their predictions, as evidenced by erasing or crossing out, after observing an event to ensure that they are correct. At this point, students struggle with the purpose of predictions and with recording them in their notebooks.

As students gain an understanding of what it means to predict, they progress by using their prior experiences when making predictions. Students may refer to previous notebook entries and provide evidence to support their thinking. Predictions begin to make sense in their entries and are not entered haphazardly. There is no longer a sense that predictions must be changed in order to be correct; rather, students revisit their predictions as they gather data and express new ideas based on evidence. They no longer equate information that does not agree with their prediction with being wrong, but rather look at it as a learning opportunity. At this point, students may need prompting from the teacher to make a prediction, as it is not yet automatic.

As students progress further, they recognize the value in recording their predictions, and predictions become a natural part of their scientific entries, as Figure 3–1 demonstrates. Although not always accurate,

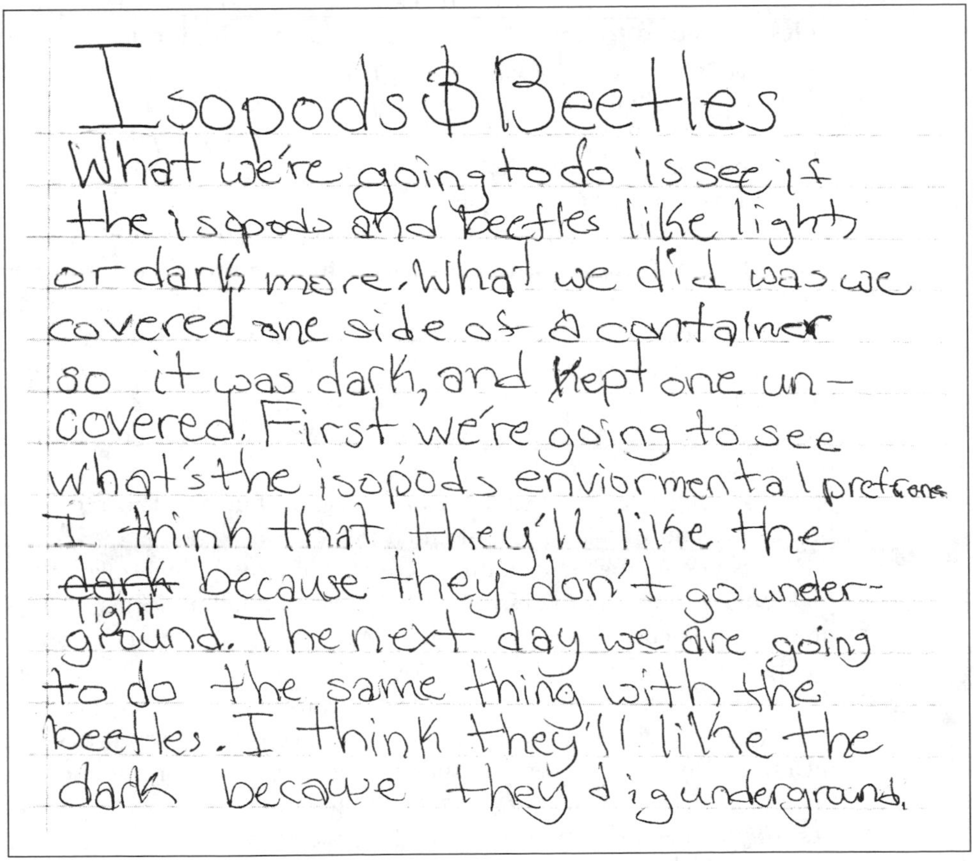

Isopods & Beetles
What we're going to do is see if the isopods and beetles like light or dark more. What we did was we covered one side of a container so it was dark, and kept one un-covered. First we're going to see what's the isopods enviormental preferons I think that they'll like the light because they don't go under-ground. The next day we are going to do the same thing with the beetles. I think they'll like the dark because they dig underground.

FIGURE 3–1 **A fifth-grade student considers what the outcome of the investigation will be.**

their predictions are supported by evidence from previous experiences with the materials. They realize that their predictions should be examined and that they should base future predictions on data collection.

Recording and Organizing Data

What evidence of progress is there in students' recording and organizing of data?

> [Students] collect data and decide how to represent it, they organize data to generate knowledge, and they test the reliability of the knowledge they have generated. (National Research Council 1996, 33)

When students begin using notebooks, they may not focus on the data as a whole but instead focus on individual pieces. Students are often busy exploring the materials and may not think to record their ideas unless prompted to do so by the teacher. Data collection may not be focused and it is often entered randomly rather than in an organized manner. This often makes it difficult to revisit information and make sense of it at a later date. Materials and procedures are often forgotten at this point and instead students focus on the results, which may be a blend of data and fictional thoughts.

After some time, students begin to show progress by experimenting with different methods of data collection; however, some may still rely on the teacher's directions for guidance with their entries. In addition to recording their ideas in lists, students may draw pictures with labels or descriptions, write sentences to describe their thinking, or create thinking maps. They begin to organize their information, using titles for their entries and grouping sections together. This organization allows them to utilize the data at a later date and build upon their understandings. Students no longer focus solely on data collection but begin to reference procedures and/or materials in their entries.

As students become more comfortable with notebooks, their method of recording progresses by taking several different forms, such as drawings, sentences, charts, and tables. As students feel more confident in their abilities to observe and record information, they often exceed the teacher's expectations. There is the realization that organization helps make sense of data, so students strive to organize their entries in a meaningful manner. Therefore, students consider the recording method prior to recording the information, and they can justify the appropriateness of one method over another. Students strive to include information in their entries so they or someone else might be able to replicate their work in the future.

> *Thinking point:* Looking at Figures 3–2 and 3–3, what can you tell about this student's progression over the course of the year?

Drawing

What evidence of progress is there in students' drawings?

> [I]nitial sketches and single-word descriptions lead to increasingly more detailed drawings and richer verbal descriptions. (National Research Council 1996, 123)

Students' drawings usually begin as symbols of objects, such as daisy-type flowers or stick figures. The symbols represent the materials but do not include details specific to the object being drawn. Students are usually familiar with drawing for enjoyment but often do not understand the significance of drawing for understanding. Therefore, materials may be drawn in imaginary scenes or color may be used inaccurately, such as coloring a mealworm purple or orange. Students may label their drawings, but they are not sure of the purpose of labels at this point and end up labeling everything on their drawings rather than specific aspects.

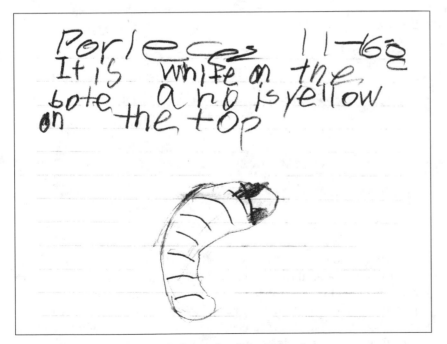

FIGURE 3–2   A second grader's notebook in September

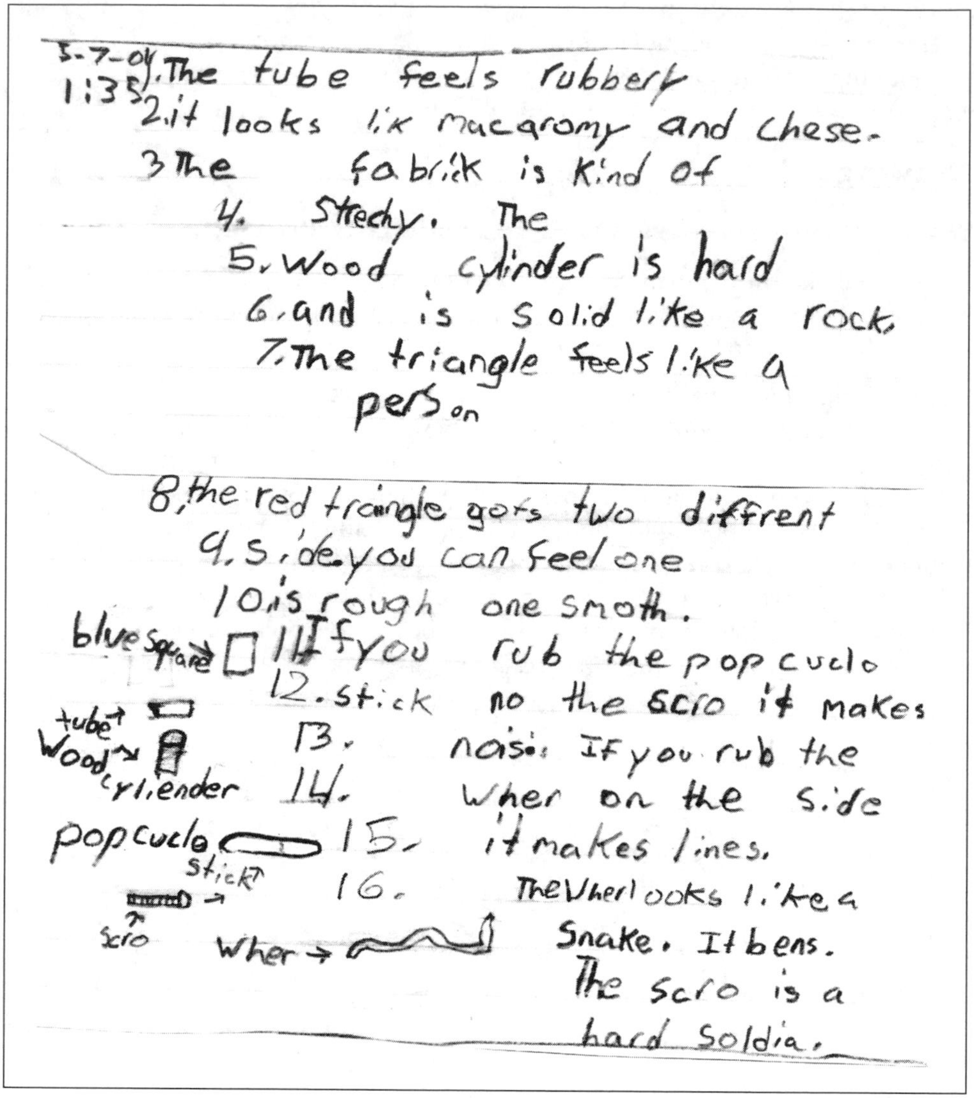

5-7-04. The tube feels rubbery
1:35 2. it looks lik macaromy and chese.
3 The   fabrik is kind of
4. Strechy. The
5. Wood cylinder is hard
6. and is solid like a rock,
7. The triangle feels like a
        person

8. the red triangle gots two diffrent
9. side. you can feel one
10. is rough one smoth.
blue square ☐ 11. If you rub the pop cuclo
        12. stick no the scro it makes
tube → ▭   13. naise. If you rub the
Wood   ▯
cyliender 14. wher on the side
popcuclo ⊂⊃   15. it makes lines.
    stick →   16.   The wher looks like a
scro → ▭▭→   Snake. It bens.
   wher → ∿∿   The scro is a
            hard soldia.

FIGURE 3–3   The same student's notebook in May

Students show progression as they begin to see drawings as learning tools. They pay attention to details, such as drawing the leaf veins or recording segments in an insect's leg. They pay attention to color and proportion for a more accurate representation of the material. They now use labels sparingly in order to clarify aspects of their drawings. There is the realization that drawing portions of the material may provide more information than drawing the entire object.

With experience, students begin using drawing techniques such as shapes and proportion, in order to provide detail in their work. They see labels as tools to enhance the drawings and define terminology. Beyond labels, students may begin to use captions in order to expand upon the entry, for example, "Bird's-eye view of isopod habitat." Students begin to manipulate the objects and may draw them from various perspectives or in different scales. They use color and shading techniques to better depict the characteristics of the object.

In the following vignette, a teacher describes how fifth-grade students progressed as they worked with drawings in their notebook entries.

Knowing that my students had had limited exposure to various drawing techniques, I was curious to see how they would record their observations as we examined plant structures. I noticed some of the drawings contained color but seemed to lack details. The plants being observed had leaves with many shades of green; however, in their notebooks many of the students colored the leaves a solid green and seemed to miss the intricate patterns created by the variation in color. The drawings also seemed to consist of the basic outlines of the plants and contained few other internal details.

As the days progressed, we utilized various techniques, such as shading, labeling, and guided drawings. Students began adding details to their drawings as we discussed specific plant features. As the study continued, their drawings became larger and they used labels to identify unique features of the plants (node, parallel veins) instead of more obvious features. Shading techniques were used, giving the drawings depth. Students began to see how powerful drawings could be in representing their understandings.

Questioning

What evidence of progress is there in students' questioning?

In the same way that scientists develop their knowledge and understanding as they seek answers to questions about the natural world, students develop an understanding of the natural world when they are actively engaged in scientific inquiry— alone and with others. (National Research Council 1996, 29)

As students work with materials, they are constantly asking questions although they may not realize it. Science notebooks become important tools for the students to capture these questions for future investigations. In the beginning, students may not be clear in recording their questions; instead, their questions are intermingled within their observations, making it difficult to distinguish them from other elements of their notebooks. Questions may go unexplored and unaddressed anywhere in their work. Questions they record may not be relevant to their investigation, as the role of questions is not clear to many students at this point.

With more experiences, students progress by beginning to recognize valuable questions. They record these in a manner that sets them apart from other elements of their notebooks. Students use techniques that allow them to quickly locate their questions, such as beginning their entries with their questions, designating a specific area of their notebooks for questions, or coding their questions in some manner. At this stage, students' questions are relevant to their investigations and may be actively pursued if time is provided. There is an understanding that questions are an important part of scientific inquiry and therefore an important component of science notebooks.

Over time, the questions that students raise are not only easy to find but may be organized in a meaningful manner as well. Students may begin grouping questions according to aspects of their investigations, such as behaviors or physical characteristics. Questions serve a purpose and are thoughtfully considered by the students as they revisit them from time to time, address them within their entries, and view them as starting points for new questions.

Reflecting

What evidence of progress is there in students' reflection upon their work?

> Students assess the efficacy of their efforts—they evaluate the data they have collected, re-examining or collecting more if necessary and making statements about the generalizability of their findings. (National Research Council 1996, 33)

When students first begin to use notebooks, they may simply record information and not interpret their findings. Students may see their notebooks as collections of data that they can look through, but they do so with the purpose of reexamining facts rather than trying to make sense of their thinking. As students share with a partner or a group, they focus on factual information. Students often look to the teacher for direction or confirmation that they are doing well, rather than relying on their own interpretation of their work.

As students become more experienced with science notebooks, they begin to see them as tools for making connections between what they are observing and their prior experiences. They no longer utilize notebooks solely for data collection; instead, they begin to synthesize their thoughts, which may include writing for several minutes after an investigation. Students attempt to explain their thinking and begin to formulate explanations, such as "I think that the sloped stream tables made deeper canyons because the water carries the deposits away faster." As students become more reflective, they recognize both patterns and inconsistencies in their data.

Using Notebooks as a Resource

What evidence of progress is there in students' use of notebooks as a resource?

> Community-centered environments require students to articulate their ideas, challenge those of others, and negotiate deeper meaning along with other learners. (National Research Council 2000, 122)

Science notebooks do not serve their true purpose unless students utilize them as resources. This is accomplished any time students refer to the information within their notebooks. For many students, referencing their notebooks helps establish a purpose for recording and organizing the information pertaining to an investigation. This can be accomplished by asking students to refer to their notebooks when discussing ideas with a partner or group. Students also reference their notebooks as they look back through their work and reflect on their understandings.

As students become more comfortable with using notebooks as a resource, they begin to reference the information within them for more formal sharing. Just as scientists present their ideas to others, students need to be encouraged to present their findings beyond their casual conversations. At the end of an investigation, students might be asked to present their findings in a more formal manner, such as a science conference, slide show, informational writing piece, or big book. The importance of having pertinent, accessible information in their notebooks takes on new meaning once the materials are no longer available for reference.

In the following vignette a teacher describes how notebooks are utilized as resources in a second-grade classroom.

> After studying the mealworm for several weeks, we had a class discussion of how we could share this information with others. One student suggested that the class could make a book. After reviewing their notebooks, the class brainstormed a list of ideas they felt should be included in the book and listed these on the

board. The students decided to take a chronological approach to sharing the information and determined that the book should focus on the life cycle of the mealworm. Students broke up into groups of four, with each group focusing on a different component of the life cycle. Within the groups, students shared tasks such as writing, drawing, and organizing their page of the book. Each page was created using information from their notebooks.

Self-Assessing

What evidence of progress is there in students' self-assessment?

> Students are the ones who must ultimately take action to bridge the gap between where they are and where they are heading. (National Research Council 2001, 17)

In order for students to fully realize the notebook's potential, they must reflect on the work they are doing to determine understandings and new goals. Students who are new to notebooks may require assistance to reflect upon their work and determine next steps to take. As they begin this process, students may assess themselves not by asking "Does the work show what I learned?" but rather "Does it look neat?" or "Did I finish?"

Eventually, goals become a focus for improving the overall notebook so that it becomes a valuable tool. For example, a student may indicate that she needs to work on organizing her data and experiment with different methods. As sole consumers of their notebooks, students continually self-assess their progress toward their goals. The students then adjust their work based upon how well they think they are meeting their goals.

Notebooks are essential components to learning science and need to be developed over time. Students will approach each of the areas discussed in this chapter in very unique ways, and they will improve their skills at various rates. It is important that students recognize the uniqueness of their notebooks and view other students' notebooks as models rather than as means of comparison.

Thinking point: How will you gather evidence of how your students are progressing within each of the areas discussed in this chapter? What opportunities will you provide to allow students to improve in each of these areas so that their notebooks support learning in science?

4

Discussions with Two Scientists

Scientists develop explanations using observations (evidence) and what they already know about the world (scientific knowledge). Good explanations are based on evidence from investigations. Scientists make the results of their investigations public; they describe the investigations in ways that enable others to repeat the investigation. Scientists review and ask questions about the results of other scientists' work. (National Research Council 1996, 123)

How Scientists Use Their Notebooks

In order to consider authentic implementation of science notebooks in the classroom, it is important to understand how scientists use notebooks in their line of work. Two scientists, Kay Rohde and Alan Gallaspy, were interviewed separately and shared ways that they have used notebooks. Kay provided insight as a national park specialist on observational fieldwork. Alan, a forensic scientist, offered information from the perspective of a controlled lab setting. We also asked the scientists to consider what is important for teachers and students to take into account when utilizing notebooks.

Please describe your job.

Kay: I am chief of interpretation for Lake Mead National Recreation Area [in Nevada and Arizona], which means that I manage all of the information and educational services in the park.

My current position does not require me to use a notebook, so I will focus on my experiences when I worked in a cave. I worked as a cave specialist for a number of years.

Alan: I am employed as a forensic scientist at one of the regional crime labs in town and usually work in the toxicology section. Toxicology is the study of the disposition and effects of poisons; most of my work is centered on drunken driving and various crimes where drugs of abuse might be involved. I also occasionally find myself testing specimens from people that have been accused in murder cases so I can better understand their thought processes at the time of the crime.

What type of notebook do you use in your work?

Kay: The science notebook we used had a slightly different purpose; it was actually a survey book with waterproof pages, because caves can get dripping wet. We had a staff logbook in which everyone would record cave conditions. Many of our entries would have a sketch with the actual readings: forward, backward, azimuth, the whole nine yards. We would also inventory resources. For each survey station, we would list everything around us and sketch the room. We also kept personal notebooks while leading cave tours, keeping watch of things in the cave, noting differences. Eventually, we used the information in the notebook to help us develop a picture of what a year in the cave looked like. We were able to document changes and use it as the basis of research later.

Alan: We are running the entire spectrum of notebooks these days. We may maintain a small spiral notebook as a record of small off-the-cuff calculations. Or, we may make some kind of notation that there is a leak in the roof that was dripping on one of the instruments to remind us to have it fixed.

   We also maintain extensive logs. For example, if we have a piece of instrumentation or some kind of analytical device, we may keep a logbook on it detailing maintenance issues, what kind of calibrations have been performed on it over time, what kind of repairs may have been made on it, when it was placed in service, and when it was taken out of service.

   We have logbooks and computer systems to help us keep track of each piece of evidence that comes in and goes out of the laboratory. We are just surrounded by paper all over the place and it can get kind of crazy at times.

What type of information do you record in your notebook and how do you organize it?

Kay: The survey book was not just my book; it was a community book. We actually taught note taking as one of the skills for working in the cave in order to maintain consistency in this community survey book. When you went in on a survey crew, you learned what and how to record. We had a tape person who measured and a note taker who could write legibly and take it all in. There was a real skill to note taking, not just getting the numbers down as the tape person called them out, but being able to sketch and record all the details.

For every surveying point we had to do a physical sketch of the room, both in cross-section as well as in plain view. The survey book became a document of everything in the cave, an inventory of it. We would go into the cave and sketch rooms including pools of water, stalactites, stalagmites, and anything else we noticed. Most of the time, it was just normal stuff and we used shorthand, indicating a feature and the size of it. But if there was something unusual, we wrote it all down and described it in detail. Unusual items might be wet spots, fossils, and things like that.

I would also go into the cave with one of the entomologists when I worked at Carlsbad [Caverns National Park in New Mexico]. He would take his own notebook into the cave and note what he found and sketch the "critters" himself. We would bait traps, he would describe their location in his notebook, and then we would go back at a later time and check the traps. He had to describe what the trap consisted of because those things could become variables in his work. When we captured insects, he would note all of the details: where the insect was found; what it looked like; conditions of the area; temperature; substrate, sometimes taking a sample of it; behavior; and time, although this might be considered irrelevant in a cave.

Alan: We spend a lot of time organizing and documenting the experiments that we are going to perform. For example, if we want to test several bloods for their alcohol level, there are a lot of things that we will do for that particular experiment. We will make a list of the samples that we will run for that particular experiment. For each of those samples, the unknowns, there will be demographical information. For example, each blood sample would have a name and maybe a case number associated with it. We might even have multiple samples from the same person drawn at different times, and we might have a number of different people all involved in one case. So we have to have some type of system to keep all of those things organized and not confuse one with the other.

In addition, if we are doing quantitative analysis, we want to have different information on where we obtained the quantitative calibrators: the manufacturer, lot number, and date of manufacture. We might have additional information on the lot numbers of different reagents used in a particular experiment. Those are just some of the elements of an experiment that we have to keep track of one way or another.

I was not by any means the first employee for that particular laboratory and there were various systems in place already. I was given a certain amount of latitude to do things my own way, but nonetheless, I was expected to comply and conform to whatever systems were currently in place. There is no sense in allowing one person to reinvent the wheel. If there is something that is known to work, to fulfill the needs of that particular institution, it makes sense to go ahead and educate others about that system.

How did you use the information in your notebooks?

Kay: A lot of the cave was sitting right under parking lots and we began to notice some trends in our notes. With the notes, we knew where all the wet places were, where there was dripping or water formations. Those notes provided us with data and became the beginnings of hydrological studies. In those studies we used dye tracing to help us make sense of the trends we were seeing. We ended up finding petrochemicals in some of the water samples, and we could directly tie the information to the parking lots, and it was the notes in our survey book that began to show us the trends.

Our notes also helped us develop a picture of the cave. We would take the numbers we recorded while underground and connect them to numbers on the top. This allowed us to actually construct a map of the cave in relationship to the surface under which it lay. With surveying, we were able to check how accurate we were with our data. When we surveyed around and the walls of the cave did not meet, we knew we had some errors in our data. Knowing this allowed us to revisit data and develop an accurate picture of the cave.

Alan: We might conduct various experiments to draw a conclusion. For example, for a drunken driver, we will analyze the quantitative level of alcohol in the person's blood and we will have the supporting data we generated for that particular sample. Based on that quantitative level, we can say whether or not someone was perhaps under the influence of alcohol while he was driving. We're fully prepared to present those findings, as more of an adversarial courtroom presentation, at that point.

Recommendations for the Classroom

Science notebooks are an essential component in the scientific community. Therefore, it is important to understand the scientists' perspective on why notebooks should be used in elementary science. This became a main component of the interview, focusing on the scientists' ideas regarding the role of notebooks in elementary science.

Why should children use science notebooks?

Kay: The main thing is to get the observations and information down; reflection will come later. If reflection is pushed too much, it will get in the way of the real purpose, which is to record the data so you can do something with it later. There needs to be a point where students think about why they did something; however, reflection should come later. The critical thing is to get the data down so it can be replicated or examined later. In a science notebook, students should be gathering information and taking notes so they can do something with the information later, such as build a map, construct an experiment, look up something, or identify a little bird.

I think that using the notebook will help kids be able to verbalize and describe. Recording in the notebook will help in vocabulary development and describing; being able to write descriptively is better in the long run no matter what they do.

Alan: You can never depend on your memory. I can't even remember what I had for breakfast this morning. If that was important, I should have recorded it in my notebook. But nonetheless, it would be foolhardy to rely on your memory for a particular experiment, no matter how simple it might be.

What are the elements that you feel are essential for student notebooks?

Kay: I think that the notebook is something that builds. Background data is essential—who, what, when, where, why, and how, particularly who, when, and what because all of that influences the investigation. With young kids, it is starting small, with very simple data, such as the temperature. As students get older they are going to figure out what else might go in there. I would probably want students to record who they are working with because that becomes important if there are questions. Then I would consider items that are specific to whatever is being investigated. Having that information helps build a picture of conditions for whatever is being done. The other thing I would want to see kids include is some questions because those are the kinds of things they go back to and say, "Hmm, let's look into that."

Alan: It is good to try to keep as much detailed and organized information as possible if you don't really know what is going to be important down the road. Completeness would account for something. You can go back from your complete notes and ascertain what was irrelevant and what was important.

What advice do you have about recording data and organizing it?

Kay: I hope teachers don't make kids write in complete sentences; they just need to get the ideas down. Everybody learns differently. Sometimes for me, just a word helps me remember; for others, they need more words or more descriptions. Let kids come up with the criteria that they need to record. It may be a collective class effort, but constantly do that so they learn what to record and they don't just rely on journaling. Journaling is fine, there is a place for it, but it will get in the way of the data collection, which is why scientists use notebooks—to record data. If scientists don't record the data, they can't replicate their work; they can't build a picture; they can't use the data if it is not complete.

Alan: The main take-home point is that it is good to anticipate, if you possibly can, what you want to record and then try to organize it in some sort of systematic way, be it a table, graph, or something along those lines. A little preparation goes a long way. There are, of course, different ways to record things; both in my work and in every scientific endeavor that I have been a part of in my life, there has been more than one way to record something.

For example, if students were making a series of observations of a seed sprouting, they would have to have some sort of organized, systematic way of recording those observations. They might have notebook entries ranging from the initial day—day one, day two—for as long as they care to run the experiment and make provisions for whatever observations they care to record in that particular space. But the key to these entries is to have an organized, systematic recording of the experiment.

Hopefully, students will be able to take a look at the data they generate with a known situation and apply that same experiment to an unknown situation and draw a conclusion from it. If they organize their notebooks properly, students should be able to do that.

What other thoughts would you like to share?

Kay: I don't ever remember using a notebook in school. I wish that someone had taught me. I think it is important to think about how students use them so it is not considered a chore but becomes natural. Maybe start with just data or just observation as a first step rather than trying to do it all. To me, having to do it all would be overwhelming as a kid.

Also, I think that it has to be real; it can't be contrived. So when doing a science project, just keep notes, time, and date—these things are automatic, kind of like putting your name, class, and period on the top right corner of the paper. I think that it is a gradual thing. Sometimes there is the expectation that a third grader will automatically have the same kind of science notebook that a premed student or biologist would have. That is one of the things that teachers need to be careful of. I think that a well-developed notebook is a gradual thing.

Alan: Careful note taking is what separates science from casual observation. For instance, I have noticed for years and years that the sun comes up over the mountain. But if I wanted to quantify that a little bit better, I would have to take very systematic notes, such as exactly which part of the mountain it comes over and if I am standing in the same spot in the valley when I make this observation.

Overall, the notebook is something that develops with time. It is like any other endeavor: you have to expose not just kids, but anyone, to a certain thing any number of times before they will get the knack of it and master it.

One of the purposes for maintaining science notebooks, in addition to exploring scientific content and literacy, is to replicate the work that scientists do. Kay and Alan have provided their perspectives on authentic use of science notebooks in two different fields of scientific study. By examining the way scientists utilize notebooks and the recommendations they have shared, teachers can develop a sense of purpose for implementing science notebooks in the classroom.

> *Thinking point:* Based upon the scientists' perspectives, how will you make science notebooks authentic for students?

5

Scientific Content and Process Connections

Learning science is something students do, not something that is done to them. (National Research Council 1996, 20)

Connections to the *National Science Education Standards*

How do science notebooks connect to the *National Science Education Standards*?

In a move to begin looking at the process of science differently, experts from across the country came together to examine what scientists do. The results of their work are the *National Science Education Standards*. "The *Standards* are the 'next word,' not the 'final word,' in our attempts to improve science programs" (Bartels 2000, 21). The *Standards* provide insight into the learning of scientific concepts and encourage teachers to provide students with opportunities to investigate and question the world around them.

In order for students to learn science, they need to be engaged in meaningful investigations with materials. The *National Science Education Standards* provide teachers with an understanding of what it looks like and means to provide students with meaningful science experiences. The *Standards* establish the students' knowledge base within eight scientific content categories:

1. unifying concepts and processes in science

2. science as inquiry

3. physical science

4. life science

5. earth and space science

6. science and technology

7. science in personal and social perspectives

8. history and nature of science

"The national standards challenge educators to move beyond 'science as a process,' in which students learn skills (observing, inferring, and hypothesizing) and to combine these skills with scientific knowledge, scientific reasoning, and critical thinking to construct a richer under-standing of science" (Bybee 1997, 11). Science notebooks provide a context in which students can use the skills Bybee talks about to construct a richer understanding of science. Science notebooks also promote five of the eight standards categories: scientific content (physical, life, and earth and space), science as inquiry, and unifying concepts and processes in science. This chapter examines the relationship between science notebooks and each of these categories.

Physical, Life, and Earth and Space Content Standards

How do science notebooks address the physical, life, and earth and space content standards?

> The important but abstract ideas of science . . . all begin with observing and keeping track of the way the world behaves. (National Research Council 1996, 126)

Scientific content refers to the information students study within physi-cal, life, and earth and space sciences. It is through content that students learn and practice the process of scientific inquiry. By utilizing notebooks in writing, discussing, and reflecting, students begin to focus on the scien-tific content they know as well as how they know it—an important step in developing students' metacognitive thinking. Students begin constructing their understandings of scientific ideas as they determine what informa-tion needs to be recorded in their notebooks and the best way to organize it. During discussions, students question one another's thinking, causing them to refer back to the evidence they collected in their notebooks to support their ideas. Reflecting in notebooks is another time when stu-dents may focus on the content they are learning. In reflecting on what worked and why it worked, students are developing conceptual under-standing. Research shows that student learning is enhanced when stu-dents are asked to write within the content areas (Reeves 2000). Notebooks provide students with one context for writing within the con-tent of science and may be used as a tool to create other forms of infor-mational writing. Chapter 6, "Literacy Connections," provides more information on other forms of informational writing that may come from science notebooks.

What evidence is there that students are learning content by using science notebooks?

Observing how students use their notebooks during an investigation and discussion can provide insight into student understanding of the content being studied. Notebooks represent the path of student knowledge—where they began and where they are currently. Students are provided with the opportunity to construct understanding while they draw, describe, create charts, and reflect. Their understanding of content is strengthened along with their recording skills.

The appearance or length of an entry may not reflect the content that is present. Some students may record very little in their notebooks or organize their information in a manner that appears to be disorganized; however, they may have a strong understanding of the content being studied. On the other hand, there are some students who may write pages upon pages in beautiful handwriting and actually say little in terms of content.

The notebooks become tools for students to help explain their thinking and justify their ideas using the evidence gathered. As students work through an investigation, they begin to make connections to prior experiences. Their notebooks become reference tools during discussions as they refer to the books to find evidence to support their thinking. In the following vignette the teacher describes how third-grade students came to an understanding of content by utilizing their notebooks in their discussions with others.

The students had been exploring pitch for some time and had several different experiences that allowed them to think about the connection between pitch and length of an item, such as metal bars or hollow tubes. Students were struggling with one of the investigations, a water xylophone, consisting of glass bottles with various amounts of water that needed to be put in order from highest to lowest pitch. I called the students to the floor to discuss this particular investigation. Students began by sharing their ideas with a partner before sharing them with the group. The first student to share with the group explained that the bottles needed to go in order from the least amount of water to the greatest and showed a picture he had drawn in his notebook to represent this. He went on to explain that the one with the most water had the highest pitch. Another student quickly disagreed and said she thought that the bottle with the smallest amount of water had the highest pitch.

In order to explore this further, we pulled the bottles out to demonstrate. The two students took turns tapping the bottles and the class agreed that each one seemed to be correct. How could this be? Another student started searching through his notebook. "I found that shorter items usually have a higher pitch, so I think the bottle with less water should have a higher pitch. This is so confusing." Students were quick to join the discussion, referring to evidence in their notebooks to support their thinking.

I listened to the conversation and realized that students had a good understanding of pitch and length, as evident by their discussion, but were getting confused with the water xylophone. From the demonstration, I realized that the two students were tapping the bottles at different locations, one above the water line and the other below. This would affect the pitch. Rather than telling students the answer, I decided to leave the water xylophone out for further investigation. We would revisit this conversation after they had more time to work with the water xylophone.

Thinking point: How will you look for evidence of content understanding when your students use their science notebooks?

Science as Inquiry

How do science notebooks address science as inquiry?

Science as inquiry "involves asking a simple question, completing an investigation, answering the question, and presenting the results to others" (National Research Council 1996, 122). As students work within an investigation, they record findings and questions in their science notebooks. Often, questions arise based on the information they have recorded. As they look back through their notebook entries, students may find that new ideas conflict with their current thinking. This conflict becomes a question and serves as a starting point for an inquiry. From that question, students plan and conduct an investigation. Based on previous data, they form a hypothesis, decide upon materials, and devise a way to find an answer. All of this is recorded in their notebooks, along with the work of the investigation. Throughout the investigation, students use their notebooks in discussions with others. When sufficient information has been gathered, students synthesize their thoughts and present their results to others through formal written or oral presentations.

Also included in this standard is the expectation that students learn how scientists conduct, document, and communicate their work. Students utilize their notebooks throughout an investigation, just as scientists do. Using science notebooks in this manner helps students develop an understanding of how scientists work and the importance of this basic, yet essential, tool to their work.

What evidence is there that students are using science as inquiry in their science notebooks?

Science as inquiry, sometimes referred to as the inquiry process, is the overarching process that students utilize to formulate an understanding of scientific content. Within science as inquiry there are five main categories, which the Exploratorium Institute for Inquiry groups as (1) observing, (2) hypothesizing, (3) planning investigations (including predictions), (4) interpreting findings and drawing conclusions, and (5) communicating (Exploraturium Institute for Inquiry 1998). This process may not be as linear as many believe, as students enter it at various stages, and evidence of science as inquiry is scattered throughout their notebooks. Understanding what the process skills may look like allows the teacher to be aware of where students are in the inquiry process.

Students' observations are recorded in a variety of ways, using drawings, lists, explanations, charts, and tables. Within their observations are wonderings and questions that lead them to new investigations. They formulate a hypothesis for their question based on successes and failures with past experiences. Using their notebooks in conversations with others becomes a natural process and a way to think about ideas. Through their work and discussions, students develop a plan for their inquiry. This plan may not be orderly and probably evolves as students work through their inquiry. Finally, students interpret their findings and present them to others either informally or formally.

In the vignette that follows, a teacher describes how a group of second-grade students utilized their notebooks as they worked through a small-group inquiry.

After exploring air resistance, students looked back through their notebooks and shared questions they had recorded while working with parachutes. I recorded these questions on the board where all the students could see them. Students then selected a question they were interested in pursuing and formed groups based on their selections. A group of three students had decided to explore how the size of the parachute affected the speed of descent.

As students began planning their inquiry, they realized that they needed to examine the parachute they used in the original investigation, as no one knew exactly how big it was and they had nothing in their notebooks about this. After looking at their original parachutes, they decided it was a regular dinner napkin and jotted this down in their notebooks. They decided that they would cut napkins to make smaller parachutes and one person suggested that they tape some napkins together to make a really big parachute. They put these ideas down in their notebooks and then called me over. Realizing that they had not formed a hypothesis yet, I asked them what they thought would happen when they tested the parachutes. They thought the smaller parachute would descend faster and referred to the times their parachute did not open, which caused it to come down very quickly. I suggested they record this in their notebooks so they could reference it later.

The group quickly began cutting and taping napkins to make different-sized parachutes and then started testing them to see what would happen. Realizing they needed a way to organize their tests, one student suggested they name each parachute so they could write about it in their notebooks. They busily went about dropping and counting how long it took each parachute to reach the ground and then recording the results in their notebooks. After testing five different-sized parachutes, one of the students commented that he didn't see much of a difference. Another student pointed out that she didn't see a big difference between each parachute, but when she looked at the results of the biggest parachute and the results of the smallest parachute, the smaller one came down faster. The students then decided to drop those two parachutes at the same time to see which one hit the ground first.

As the small groups wrapped up their inquiries, we came back together as a whole class to share our findings. The class listened intently as each group shared what they had learned in a short presentation. Many groups showed the parachutes they had made to the group and used evidence from their notebooks to support their findings.

Thinking point: How will you look for evidence of science as inquiry when your students use their science notebooks?

Unifying Concepts and Processes

How do science notebooks address unifying concepts and processes?

In elementary science, students are learning to make sense of the unifying concepts and processes. These are the skills that allow students to create a bigger picture by examining the information they have gathered through small units of study. For example, by using the unifying concepts and processes, students are able to apply information they learned about four various insects to identify characteristics that are common to all insects.

Science notebooks are authentic tools that students use to work with the ideas presented within this category and bring together their science experiences. Within notebooks, students begin to make sense of the concepts included in the *National Science Education Standards*: "systems, order, and organization"; "evidence, models, and explanation"; and "constancy, change, and measurement." As students work in a content area, their notebooks allow them to build connections between the unifying concepts and processes and the content being studied.

The first concept deals with system, order, and organization. Through examining notebook entries, students are able to begin thinking about the various components of the systems they are working with and the connections that exist between them. A sense of order begins to emerge, allowing students to bring organization to the concept with which they are working and to the ideas represented within their notebooks.

The second concept focuses on evidence, models, and explanation. While working in science, students are gathering evidence of their thinking in their science notebooks. Through observation or experimentation, students gather evidence as drawings, explanations, and/or data to use in support of their scientific explanations. Models help students make sense of how things work. Models are represented in notebooks as plans, equations, drawings, and so on. Students use models to support their scientific explanations. When forming hypotheses or conclusions, students base their explanations on information recorded in their notebooks.

Constancy, change, and measurement require students to look at materials over time. By keeping notebooks, students are able to look at an object through various stages of an inquiry and note changes that take place or aspects of the material that remain constant. Notebooks allow students to keep track of measurements and determine what would be considered appropriate based on past experiences. Notebooks provide students with a quick and easy means to access information over time, allowing them to have the experiences necessary to gain an understanding of concepts.

What evidence do notebooks provide that students are making sense of the unifying concepts and processes?

Students' understanding grows with time and is represented within their entries. They begin to make connections between concepts and refer to past experiences to help explain new ideas. Evidence becomes an important component of their entries, and during discussion they ask each other on what evidence their ideas are based. Change is represented in their entries and they realize the importance of dating each entry in order to reference the time that has elapsed. It is the concepts presented in this standard that allow students to begin making connections between ideas and applying them to other situations.

In the following vignette a teacher describes how first graders utilized their notebooks in examining the system of balance.

> I challenged my students to create a balanced system using a craft stick, pencil, wire, and clothespins. The pencil was to balance on its sharpened tip on the end of the craft stick. From past experiences, they knew that the clothespins, or counterweights, could be used to make an object balance. I saw some students look back at their notes to see how they had balanced cardboard figures, while others started immediately with the materials. Soon all of them were wrapping the wire around the pencil and attaching the clothespins at various points to see if they could get the pencil to balance. As some students began creating the balanced system, other students observed what they were doing differently and it wasn't long before everyone had managed to create a balanced system. I gave them a few minutes to make sure they had recorded their systems in their notebooks before calling them to the floor for a group discussion. We examined the various systems that were created and discussed what would happen if we made changes to them. I wanted students to think about the systems and how important each part was to the system, a unifying concept.

Thinking point: How will you look for evidence that your students are using the unifying concepts and processes when they use their science notebooks?

In order to meet Bybee's challenge of taking students beyond learning "science as a process," teachers must employ methods that replicate the work of scientists. Notebooks are essential tools to scientists and therefore need to be considered as essential to the learning of elementary science. Notebooks, while developing literacy, help students make connections to the larger scientific concepts that they will build on throughout the rest of their education.

> *Thinking point:* How will you meet Bybee's challenge of taking students beyond learning science as a process and increase students' learning of scientific content?

Literacy Connections

*Both research and practical experience demonstrate that language is an
essential part of science learning and that both native English speakers
and English Language Learners develop their language skills through
authentic experiences. (Bybee 2002, 41)*

Connections to Literacy

How do science notebooks promote literacy?

Literacy is defined in a broader sense today than it has been in the past.
"For many years, literacy was defined in a very limited way—as the ability to read or write one's own name . . . A much more ambitious definition of literacy today includes the capacity to accomplish a wide range of
reading, writing, and other language tasks associated with everyday life"
(National Council of Teachers of English and International Reading
Association 1996, 4). Science notebooks promote critical language use
among students as they utilize the skills of questioning, hypothesizing,
and reflecting. This chapter focuses on the role of notebooks within
three areas of literacy: oral communication, writing, and reading.

Oral Communication

How do science notebooks promote literacy in terms of oral communication?

Children have a variety of reasons for talking in classroom settings. They talked to respond to questions posed by the teacher,
to obtain answers to their own queries, to get assistance from
peers and their teachers, to learn how to accomplish tasks, to
participate with their peers and to understand why things hap-
pened as they did. (Fullerton 1995, 11)

Throughout an investigation, students are encouraged to discuss ideas with partners, in small groups, and/or with the entire class. This oral communication—science talk—allows them to make sense of their thinking, share their ideas with others, and receive feedback. It is talk that helps students "bridge new concepts and clarify thought" (Fullerton 1995, 16). As students work through an investigation, they talk informally as they record data and observations in their notebooks, which they then bring to the group for a more formal discussion. Often, it is in sharing their evidence with others during science talk that students begin to make sense of a concept and connect information in their notebooks to bigger ideas.

For some students, science talk is an essential precursor to writing in their science notebooks. Some students may even engage in self-talk when confronted with a difficult concept. Through this self-talk, students explore, predict, and analyze their work as they communicate with themselves. Putting ideas down in black and white can be scary for students who are exploring new concepts, as writing adds a dimension of permanence. Talk, on the other hand, feels safer because ideas are dis-

FIGURE 6–1   Two students discuss science concepts using their science notebooks.

cussed but are not permanently recorded. "Since talk assists learning, teachers must maximize talk opportunities for children" (Fullerton 1995, 16). Providing these opportunities will assist students in feeling more secure, and as students feel secure in their thinking, they may be more open to recording their thinking in their notebooks.

> *Thinking point:* How will you incorporate science talk in your classroom?

Written Communication

How do science notebooks help promote written communication during science investigations?

Experiences provide a foundation for students to develop language; by engaging students in inquiry-based science, teachers are supporting this development. Therefore, there is a natural link between science notebooks and language development. Use of notebooks provides students with an authentic reason to write in science, and communicating ideas encourages students to synthesize their thinking in order to share it with others. Writing in science allows students to write about something with which they are familiar.

As scientists work, they record their information in their science notebooks. For some students, recording while working is a difficult task. The excitement of an investigation may make it difficult for some to stop and record in their notebooks; however, it is essential that they work toward being able to do this. When students are exposed to an integration of notebooks and the scientific investigations, recording while they work becomes second nature.

Recording during an investigation takes practice and may require support. There are some simple strategies that teachers can consider to prompt writing in the notebooks:

- Suggest students record the information in their notebooks, as they might find it useful later.
- Ask students to look at their notebooks during an investigation to see if they reflect all that they have learned. If not, ask students to take a few minutes to record that important information.
- Set the stage before students are expected to record in their notebooks. This can be accomplished by asking students to think about what or how they might want to record in their notebooks before beginning the investigation.

Students at the beginning stages of writing may find it easier to record with drawings. Technical drawings can be powerful tools for students at this stage to share their conceptual understandings; see Chapter 2, "Elements of a Science Notebook," for more information on technical drawings. As mentioned earlier, some students find it helpful to talk about their investigation before writing, as this allows their ideas to come to the forefront. Students may feel that they need to record in complete sentences; however, changes in science occur quickly and it may be easier to capture this information with phrases and lists rather than complete sentences. Teachers should encourage various recording methods that allow students to capture the essence of the science. The goal of science notebooks is a deeper understanding of science content; it is important that this remains the goal and that writing elements (punctuation, grammar) do not get in the way of this learning.

Through using notebooks on a regular basis, students should become comfortable with recording in their notebooks and using various recording strategies. Eventually, students should be able to select a recording strategy that works best for the data they are gathering, whether that method is pictures, lists, phrases, graphs, tables, or sentences.

Thinking point: How will you promote writing in science notebooks during an investigation?

How do science notebooks help promote written communication after the science investigation?

> Writing in notebooks and discussions reflect the most reasonable syntheses of data and conclusions drawn from individual and group experience. Then, findings are formalized in a report, presentation, and/or publication that is clear and honed—the final product of the work. (Bybee 2002, 42)

Throughout an investigation, students may reflect on their work, examine their evidence, and write about their ideas in order to clarify their thinking. When students are ready to share their findings with others, they refer to the information in their notebooks to create products (writing, slide shows, posters, oral presentations). These products provide students with an authentic opportunity to practice informational writing; therefore, the focus of scientific products should be on sharing the information in a nonfiction manner.

> Many scientists present their research at annual conferences. (Olson and Cox-Peterson 2001, 43)

Just as scientists share their findings, students are also encouraged to do so in science conferences. The science conference is an opportunity for students to present and justify their understandings to other students or adults. It allows students to practice the skills of writing, speaking, and listening in the context of science. When discussing the science conference, Olson and Cox-Peterson stated this activity "allowed students to share their research in a manner consistent with how scientists share their research. The students felt the conference was more meaningful than a project or report completed for the class, largely due to the authentic audience" (2001, 43).

> *Thinking point:* How will students formalize the information in their science notebooks to share it with a broader community?

Reading

How do science notebooks help promote reading?

> In this Information Age the importance of being able to read and write informational texts critically and well cannot be overstated. Informational literacy is central to success, and even survival, in advanced schooling, the workplace, and the community. (Duke 2000, 202)

Science notebooks serve as another tool the teacher has in promoting informational literacy among students, as the data and evidence students are collecting fits this category. Student-generated writing can be a powerful motivator for beginning or reluctant readers, as it is their language and therefore highly readable. By asking students to reread their notebook entries, the teacher is encouraging them to work with informational text at their level. After using notebooks as a beginning stage of reading, students can progress to other related informational text.

After an investigation, students use other printed information for various reasons. One reason may be to verify their findings. Another reason may be to research questions that they were unable to answer through their investigations, as some questions lend themselves more to research than to inquiry. A third reason may be to see what others have to say about the materials they have been working with, as much of elementary science is the exploration of developed concepts. Finally, printed materials may also be used to raise new questions. After an investigation, students are prepared to be critical readers because they are to some degree now experts themselves. They question text rather than accept everything they see in print. This questioning may motivate students to return to the materials in order to investigate ideas about which they read but of which they are not entirely convinced. Based on their reading, students may choose to add information to their notebooks.

In the vignette that follows, a teacher describes how second-grade students used their experiences as a basis for the critical examination of a book.

> After several days of working with solids, students created and recorded a working definition for the term *solid*, which became part of our class word bank. They defined a solid as an object that can hold its shape without a container. During reading I introduced books about solids based upon the work they had done in science. As students read these books during our independent reading time, they were engaged, looking at what others said about solids. One of the students came to me with a book in his hand and a puzzled look on his face.
>
> "This book's definition for a solid is different than what we said."
>
> "Why do you say that?"
>
> "It says that a solid is a hard object. I know that feathers and fabrics are solid objects, but they don't fit this definition."
>
> This student was using his experiences in class to think critically about the material he was now reading.

The next vignette describes how a teacher working with a group of third graders used literature to help them answer their research questions.

> Throughout the investigation of crayfish, students had recorded questions in their notebooks. Some of these pertained to information they wanted to know but would be difficult to investigate in a classroom setting. As the investigation started coming to an end, we looked back at our questions and determined which ones we had not found answers to at this point. Some of their questions included What is the natural habitat like? What do crayfish eat in their natural habitat? and How are the crayfish able to regenerate their claws? I suggested that other scientists had studied crayfish, too, and we might refer to what they learned to help us answer these questions. I introduced a variety of books on crayfish and other crustaceans. As students read and found answers to their questions, they added this information to their notebooks.

> *Thinking point:* What opportunities can you provide for students to
> connect their notebooks to reading?

Vocabulary Development

What is the role of science notebooks in vocabulary development?

Science notebooks also aid in the development of vocabulary. While
vocabulary is not the main focus of notebooks, it is a by-product of their
use. Within science, vocabulary is developed in the context of the investigation. As students begin writing in their notebooks, they use language
with which they are familiar to describe the work they are doing.
Throughout the investigation, the students' informal language is connected to the formal scientific vocabulary by both the teacher and other
students. Some students may record this in their notebooks while others
may not. As students continue to work through an investigation, they
may begin to include the formal scientific vocabulary as an integral part
of the oral and written language. Figure 6–2 shows how a student has
included formal vocabulary in her writing.

Science vocabulary is learned within the context of the investigation
and recorded in notebooks in a similar manner. As students become
comfortable with the formal vocabulary and make sense of it, they incorporate it into their notebooks naturally. The notebooks provide students
with an opportunity to use vocabulary in a contextual manner. Notebooks should not become a place where students copy vocabulary words
along with their definitions. This does little to demonstrate how well they
understand the words; rather, it demonstrates that they can copy. Eventu-

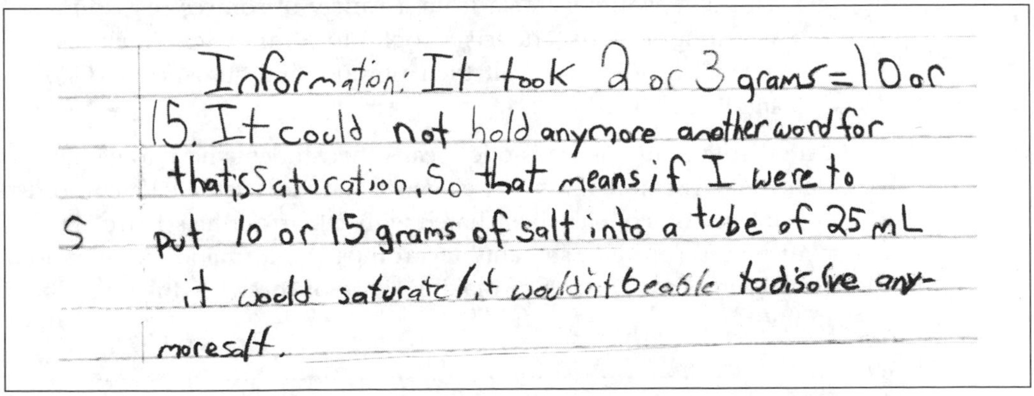

> Information: It took 2 or 3 grams = 10 or
> 15. It could not hold anymore another word for
> that;s Saturation. So that means if I were to
> S put 10 or 15 grams of salt into a tube of 25mL
> it would saturate/it wouldn't be able to disolve any-
> moresalt.

FIGURE 6–2   A fifth-grade student demonstrates understanding of vocabulary by embedding
it in her notebook entry.

ally, students should understand the vocabulary well enough to be able to use it in the correct context while speaking and writing.

Connections to the *Standards for the English Language Arts*

What connections are there between science notebooks and the *Standards for the English Language Arts*?

> Students employ a wide range of strategies as they write and use different writing process elements appropriately to communicate with different audiences for a variety of purposes. (NCTE and IRA 1996, 35)

Many times students write for others; however, within their notebooks, they are writing for their own needs and using the information they collect to share with others. Writing in their notebooks allows them "to understand the varying demands of different kinds of writing tasks and to recognize how to adapt tone, style, and content for the particular task at hand" (NCTE and IRA 1996, 35).

Writing about science provides students with a real purpose based on firsthand experiences. Research shows that "students' ability to create text . . . is best developed through engagement in meaningful reading and writing activities" (NCTE and IRA 1996, 36). Just as scientists record their daily work, students need to record their daily work. By asking students to then utilize their recordings, teachers provide them with the meaningful experience that is important in showing students the value of writing.

> Students conduct research on issues and interests by generating ideas and questions, and by posing problems. They gather, evaluate, and synthesize data from a variety of sources (e.g., print and nonprint texts, artifacts, people) to communicate their discoveries in ways that suit their purpose and audience. (NCTE and IRA 1996, 37)

An experience in science is one means that students have to gather evidence and assemble ideas. The evidence and ideas gathered are recorded in students' notebooks, then shared with others during science talk and conferences. For many students, recording the information in their notebooks serves as a means of making sense of the work they have been doing.

> *Thinking point:* How do science notebooks help address your literacy standards as set forth by your state or district?

Besides building scientific content and replicating the work that scientists do, great potential exists for notebooks to support the development of literacy through reading, writing, and speaking. The true potential of science notebooks will be realized when teachers provide "students with opportunities to read, write, and speak as scientists; attaching purpose to the use of print materials; and making the conventions and forms of reading, writing, and speaking in science explicit" (DiGisi 1998, 3). When used to their full potential, science notebooks help promote the idea that science is a context for literacy development.

Thinking point: What role will science notebooks play in literacy development within your classroom?

Appendix

Sample Student Notebook Pages

Then the invisable air blows it and it turns
it. It turns it self because the air and
the flaps make it go down then it
turnes it self. Or what I think is
because the paper clip makes it heavy.
I think when you take of the paper
clip it spins a little bit slow. And
when it is on the side of the
whirlygig it spins faster. The blue square
is soft and you can see through it.
You can stretch it but not far.
The wood cylinder is a solid and.
is hard. It's rolled and you can
roll it. It has to circles on the sides.
The traingle is benable and it
feels like plastic gum you eat.
And it has 3 sides and corners.
The plastic tube bends. It is smooth
and you can blow through it and
it is not heavy. It is transperented.
You can stand it up and
it will stay on your table.

Pages from a second grader's notebook

The wire can bend and it is skinny. It is white and gold in the inside. The screw has bumps on the stick part. And it has a line on the top of the cirle that is on the top. The popcicle stick is straight and it can brake if you crack it. And if you put it on the line it will stay

I used the cup, traingle, tube, wire, screw, rubber band, card bord. But I didn't use the aluminim foil because I didn't have know were to put it on. I made it by pating a hole in the cup. Then I put the stran in there. Then I put the tube on the straw so I could put the screw on. Then I put the blue napkin on. Then I put the red traingle on then I showed Mr. Campbell.

Soilds & Water   June 22, 2001
   Predictions
           Rock Salt
1   I think the ↑ will dusove all
    the salt. I think the
    dark rocks will be light
    like the other ones. I
    think that all the dark
    suff will dusove
    off.

_____

    Questions
2
    Is the salt going to dusove
    in the water? What color
    would it trunewien it is
    in the water.
    That the rock salt is dusovei
    and the black suff. is
    dasoveing off. and black
    and salt are sticking too
    the bodm,
         22

Pages from a third grader's notebook

before

rock salt

That the rock—
salt was vanshing
out of the cup
it was salt and
black suff
that was in
it. That when
you look throth
the monefloin
glass it is very
helpful too use
because you
see more.

cup

popscile
stick

rock
salt

23

Mini gut Bucket   5-1-02
When   we   tided   the   clip
to   the   string   on   the   chair
and   pulled   the   string   and   pull
it   sounds   like   a   gatar.
There   was   alot   of
tension. When   you   do   the
same   thing   put   it   has
tap - tap   sound. I   thing
it   does   that   because
when   you   pull   it   tight
and   when   you   don't   pull
it   tight   it   has   a
lower   sound   and
when   it's   tight   it
makes   a   higher   sound.
Tension   is   how   tight   er
how   lous   it   is.

Pages from a fourth grader's notebook

Questions   May 1, 2002
My question is what
would happen if I got the
tunning fork and hit it
on the wood then hit it on
the popsicle stick?

Sound Investigation

Under the water it sounds
lound because when you tap
the ege of the bucket
it sounds like the pool
some one splashing or
Some one jumped in the pool.
My Question is what would
happen if I put the stethosope
in the water? Under the
water you can hear
people doing
Something or hear
people moving.

KoolAIDE

~~Kool AID~~

Cup I = 1 scoop of Kool-AID
Cup J = 3 scoops of Kool-AID
1 scoop = 25 mil.
Going to dump 1,000 ml. into
each cup. He will stir. I
think that cup I will be
not as sweet as cup J.
J I think will be really sweet
Mr. Campbell will pour I into
cup A. J into cup B.

~~A~~	~~B~~
not clean	more red
redish/orange	smells stronger then A
	Bolder

Pages from a fifth grader's notebook

"B" is stronger, bolder, and redder then "A" because it has more scoops of Kool-AID. This is a mixture.
I̲s cup B a solution?
Obviesly A is not a solution because we have a cup w/ more Kool-AID. A/B are both mixtures. Yes it is a solution because you can't see any more particles floating in water.
Are all mixtures aren't a solution because the rocks and water were a mixture but not a solution because it didn't dissolve all the way.

Definition

Consitrated-darker, more stuff in it.
Daluted-lighter, less stuff in it,

Definition

Bibliography

Bartels, Dennis. 2000. "An introduction to the *National Science Education Standards.*" In *Foundations: Inquiry: Thoughts, Views, and Strategies for the K–5 Classroom.* Arlington, VA: National Science Foundation.

Bybee, Rodger W. 1997. *Achieving Scientific Literacy.* Portsmouth, NH: Heinemann.

Bybee, Rodger W., ed. 2002. *Learning Science and the Science of Learning.* Arlington, VA: NSTA Press.

DiGisi, L. L. 1998. "Summary of CUSER Institute on Science and Literacy." Education Development Center, Inc., Newton, MA. [Online]. Available: *www2.edc.org/cse/pdfs/products/literacy.pdf.*

Duke, Nell K. 2000. "3.6 Minutes per Day: The Scarcity of Informational Texts in First Grade." *Reading Research Quarterly* 35 (2): 202–24.

Dyasi, Rebecca. 2002. Conversation with authors. Las Vegas, NV, 13 June.

Exploratorium Institute for Inquiry. 1998. "The Process Circus: Developing the Process Skills of Inquiry-Based Science." [Online]. Available: *www.exploratorium.edu/ifi/activities/processcircus/circusfulltext.html.*

Fullerton, Olive. 1995. "Using Talk to Help Learn Mathematics." *English Quarterly* 27 (4): 10–16.

Gallaspy, Alan. 2002. Interview by authors. Tape recording. Las Vegas, NV, 14 September.

Moline, Steve. 1995. *I See What You Mean: Children at Work with Visual Information.* York, ME: Stenhouse Publishers.

National Council of Teachers of English (NCTE) and International Reading Association (IRA). 1996. *Standards for the English Language Arts.* Urbana, IL: National Council of Teachers of English.

National Research Council. 1996. *National Science Education Standards.* Washington, DC: National Academy Press.

————. 2000. *Inquiry and the National Science Education Standards: A Guide for Teaching and Learning.* Washington, DC: National Academy Press.

————. 2001. *Classroom Assessment and the National Science Education Standards.* Washington, DC: National Academy Press.

Olson, Joanne, and Anne M. Cox-Peterson. 2001. "An Authentic Science Conference." *Science and Children* 38 (6): 40–45.

Reeves, Douglas B. 2000. Teaching and Learning in the Clark County: Keys to Successful Student Achievement. Center for Performance Assessment, Denver, Colorado. Duplicated.

Rohde, Kay. 2002. Interview by authors. Tape recording. Las Vegas, NV, 5 October.